EXPERIENCING UNION WITH GOD THROUGH INNER PRAYER
& THE WAY AND RESULTS OF UNION WITH GOD

MADAME JEANNE GUYON

EXPERIENCING UNION WITH GOD THROUGH INNER PRAYER
& THE WAY AND RESULTS OF UNION WITH GOD

REVISED IN MODERN ENGLISH BY
HAROLD J. CHADWICK

Bridge-Logos

Gainesville, Florida 32614 USA

Unless otherwise indicated, all Scripture quotations in this publication are from the King James Version of the Bible.

Scripture quotations marked NKJV are from the New King James Version. Copyright ©1979, 1980, 1982, Thomas Nelson Inc., Publishers. Used by permission.

Experiencing God / Prayer (2 Vols.)
by Madame Guyon
Copyright © 2001 by Bridge Logos
International Standard Book Number: 0-88270-873-2
Library of Congress Catalog Card Number: Pending
Reprinted 2004

Published by:
Bridge-Logos
Gainsville, Florida, FL 32614, USA
bridgelogos.com

TABLE OF CONTENTS

FOREWORD

This is the tenth Christian classic that I've revised, and it has been the most difficult one of all. Having read and followed the teachings of many deeper life books, I understand Madame Guyon's concept of inner prayer and ultimate union of the soul with God—and like Fénelon agree with much that she wrote.

But when Madame Guyon wrote her book on inner prayer in the mid-1600s, and later her letter to Fénelon to try to clarify to him what she wrote, she was writing about a way to God that had not been generally practiced in the Church for hundreds of years. So she had to develop new expressions and combinations of words to express it. She also used common words to mean something that they did not ordinarily, or perhaps ever before, mean—hoping, I'm sure, that in the context of what she wrote, and with sufficient meditation, they would be understood. And in her day they certainly seemed to be, for thousands read her book all over France and Europe. So much so that it eventually put her into prison for seven years.

Now the way to union with God through inner prayer had never totally left the Church, as nothing that is truly of God ever does. But from the time of the apostle Paul only a few certain highly spiritual

Christians, and some monks and mystics, had ever found it for themselves. And none of them ever wrote about it for the general mass of people as Madame Guyon did. By that time, however, the church to which she belonged ruled the secular world and was filled with rituals and traditions and hundreds of external religious rules and activities with which it burdened the people and kept them in bondage to it.

Then along came Madame Jeanne Guyon with a book on a simple and easy method of inner prayer that ultimately leads to union of the soul with God. Not long after it was published, the religious leaders of her church could well have said about her what was said about Paul and Silas, "This woman has turned our world upside down."

Here is how her book was published, in her own words:

"Among my intimate friends was a civilian, a counselor of the Parliament of Grenoble, who might be described as a model of piety. Seeing on my table my manuscript treatise on Prayer, he desired me to lend it to him. Being much pleased with it, he lent it to some of his friends. Others wanted copies of it. He resolved, therefore, to have it printed. The proper ecclesiastical permissions and approbations were obtained. I was requested to write a Preface, which I did.

"Under these circumstances this book, which within a few years, passed through five or six editions, was given to the world. The Lord has given a great blessing to this little treatise; but it has caused great excitement among those who did not accede to its principles, and has been the pretence of various trials and persecutions which I have endured.

"Books are God's instruments of good as well as sermons. He who cannot preach may talk; and he who cannot do either, may perhaps write. A good book, laid conscientiously upon God's altar, is no small thing."

In this book I've included a great amount of Madame Guyon's original words and text, so that you may decide for yourself if I have correctly and clearly revised her writing into modern English. I hope you will find it so, and that you will also consider this "a good book." Here and there throughout the book I have added a word or words to hopefully clarify Madame Guyon's text—they are enclosed in brackets [like this].

If there was a prayer that could sum up all that is in this book, and that would be an excellent prayer for each of us who seek the deeper life and ultimate union of our soul with God, it would be a prayer that Kathryn Kuhlman prayed constantly. I offer it to you for your use and the principle and goal of your journey into God.

Not some of Thee, and some of me;
But all of Thee, and none of me.

Harold J. Chadwick

GOD'S REFINER: MADAME JEANNE GUYON

In his devotional commentary on "Genesis," Matthew Henry wrote that man was dust refined, but woman, being taken out of man, was dust "double refined." In thus saying, Henry sensed the purpose of God in so creating the nature of a woman that He could use her to refine His people. One of the most famous and influential of "God's Refiners" was Madame Jeanne Guyon.

Madame Guyon was born Jeanne Marie Bouvier de la Motte on April 18, 1648. Although she had wealthy parents and later was married to an even wealthier man, her life was filled with hardships and persecutions because of her determination to love God with all of her being. Like Paul, her heart hungered to "know Him,"[1] and she pursued Christ with a fervent love all the days of her life. And like Paul, increasing experiences in Jesus Christ brought her such contentment and peace that not even illness, privation, or prison could take them from her. Indeed, it was out of those very hardships that she learned that if there is no rest in God, there is no rest anywhere.

From age four to fifteen, Jeanne was in several religious seminaries where she was placed by her pious father. In one of them she found a Bible someone left behind and literally devoured it. This formed a lifelong habit of Bible study in an age when Bible reading was discouraged by the Roman Catholic Church to which she belonged. Even with this, Jeanne's spiritual life vacillated during her early years, especially as she developed into a strikingly beautiful young lady. She acquired a "peevish attitude," often "went several days without thinking of God," and began "to pass a good deal of my time before my mirror."[2]

Just before her sixteenth birthday, her father arranged a marriage between her and M. Jacques Guyon, a 38-year-old man of great wealth. Although there were several young men nearer her own age to whom Jeanne was attracted and would have preferred in marriage, her father ignored her desires, possibly because of Guyon's large fortune. So Jeanne set aside her own desires and in obedience to her father's request, but with great sorrow, she signed the articles of marriage, without being permitted to know what they were, on January 28, 1664. She did not meet her "spouse-elect in Paris until two or three days before" their marriage on March 21, 1664. From that time on she was known as Madame Jeanne Guyon.

In her autobiography, Jeanne wrote about her wedding day, "the joy of our nuptials was universal through our village. Amid this general rejoicing, there appeared none sad but myself. I could neither laugh as others did, nor even eat; so much was I depressed. I did not know the cause. It was a foretaste that God gave me of what was to befall me. "

It was when she was pregnant with her second child that God opened her heart to the glories of the mystery, "which is, Christ in you." Of that moment, she wrote in her autobiography, "I had often spoken to my confessor[3] about the great anxiety it gave me to find I could not meditate, nor exert my imagination in order to pray. Subjects of prayer which were too extensive were useless to me. Those which were short and pithy suited me better.

"At length, God permitted a very religious person . . . to pass by my father's dwelling. At my father's urging . . . I spoke to him of my difficulties about prayer. He replied, 'It is, Madame, because you seek without what you have within. Accustom yourself to seek God in your heart, and you will find Him.'

"Having said these words, he left me. They were to me like the stroke of a dart, which penetrated through my heart. I felt a very deep wound, a wound so delightful that I desired not to be cured. These words brought into my heart what I had been seeking so many years. Rather they discovered to me what was there, and which I had not enjoyed for want of knowing it."

Love poured from her heart with a new purity. "The taste of God was so great," she wrote, "so pure, unblended and uninterrupted, that it drew and absorbed the power of my soul into a profound recollection without act or discourse. I had now no sight but of Jesus Christ alone. All else was excluded in order to love with the greatest extent, without any selfish motives or reasons for loving."

As the years passed, she developed faith in God for everything. Not only for salvation, but for every material necessity and every situation and circumstance in her life. She literally abandoned herself to God. "Great faith," she wrote, "produces great abandonment." No matter what happened to her, she saw it all as the hand of God ridding her of her self-life so that the resurrected life of Christ could have predominance in her. Practical and complete inner peace was possible for everyone, Madame Guyon believed, lived, and taught. And all this, she insisted, was obtainable *by faith* alone, and not by any external works or religious ceremonies or rituals.

About 1685, she wrote the book you are now reading on how to experience union with God through prayer. It was then titled, *A Short and Very Easy Method of Prayer*. At a time when her church was stringent in its dogma that salvation and advancement in religion were through external ceremonies and duties and almost abusive self-denial, her book, teaching that true advancement in God was *internal* and was by faith alone created a storm. In one town, an enthusiastic Frenchman distributed 1500 copies of her book from door to door. In another town, an incensed church official forcefully removed 300 copies from homes and burned them.

From the day this book was first published, and for the rest of her life, Madame Guyon was either proclaimed for her teachings or denounced as a heretic wherever she went. Eventually, this book, plus her commentary on the "Song of Solomon," was given to the king of France, Louis 14th, as evidence that she should be arrested.

In 1695 she was tried and sentenced to seven years in prison. For the first three years she was kept in a prison in Vincennes, then in 1698, she was transferred to solitary confinement in the infamous French Bastille in Paris. It has been said that in the cell next to her was the famous "prisoner in the iron mask," who was rumored to be Louis the Fourteenth's twin brother, who he imprisoned for fear he would someday wrest the crown from him.

The damp, unheated, and poorly ventilated cell where she was confined so weakened Madame Guyon's always frail constitution that she remained in ill health the rest of her life. Few could have withstood, even as well as she did, those long, solitary, hours, the days and nights that could hardly be distinguished from each other, the damp walls, the cold of the winters, and the blistering heat of the summers. Her only view of the outside world for four years was a high small window that showed a bit of the sky during the day and a few stars at night. Her only food and clothing were whatever she or her friends could pay for and the guards did not steal. Of her imprisonment someone wrote, "Her only crime was loving God."

Madame Guyon spent four years in the Bastille. She was released from there in 1702. At the time of her liberation, she was fifty-four years old. When she was first released, she was allowed to visit her daughter, the Countess of Vaux, who lived either in Paris or in the immediate vicinity. But the people connected with her personal history and name were so many in that area, and so strong was the influence she was still capable of exerting, that she was only permitted to remain there for a short time. Though she had already suffered so much for her teachings, afflictions continued to be pressed upon her in a new form. The sorrows of a distant exile followed the anguish of four years of solitary confinement, during which she was not allowed contact with any of her family, friends, or acquaintances.

She was banished by Louis 14th to Blois, a large city one-hundred miles southwest of Paris, on the Loire river. The banishment was for life, and she was warned that if she ever left that city she would be returned to the Bastille for the rest of her life. She remained in Blois until her death fifteen years later on June 9, 1717, at the age of sixty-nine. Her banisher, Louis 14th, died two years before she did.

During her years at Blois, thousands traveled to her home to sit at her feet and be taught the inner life of peace and contentment through inner pray and absolute trust in God for everything. Exile could not silence the apostle John, and neither could it silence Madame Guyon. Until a few weeks before her death, she wrote daily to others, encouraging and guiding them in their spiritual quest. While at Blois she also completed her autobiography, which was written in obedience to the commands of her director, Father La Combe. That book alone has inspired hundreds-of-thousands to seek the deeper life.

During her lifetime, Madame Guyon wrote forty books—paraphrases of several of them are now available. Though dead almost three hundred years, yet she lives, to inspire, to encourage, to refine. Only God knows how many trace their deeper-life experiences to her life and teachings.

There is no doubt that she gave birth to much of the piety and holiness that characterized the life and doctrines óf John Wesley—who personally translated her book from the original French into English—and, consequently, the early Methodists. About her, Wesley wrote, "We may search many centuries before we find another woman who was such a pattern of true holiness. How few such instances do we find of exalted love to God, and our neighbor; of genuine humility; of invincible meekness, and of unbounded resignation."

The fire of God that burned in Jeanne Guyon lit fires in others who burned almost equally bright. Among her enthusiastic admirers were Count Zinzendorf, leader of the Moravians, who were the first missionaries. The early Quakers and their leader George Fox. The renowned Christian writer Jesse Penn-Lewis. Hudson Taylor, who founded the "Inland China Mission" and established one-thousand faith missions in China. Watchman Nee had her book on prayer translated into Chinese for distribution to all new converts of "The Little Flock." Paul Billheimer, the late author of "Destined for the Cross," said only the apostle Paul and Madame Guyon truly exemplified the life of Jesus.

In a harsh age of hardships and persecution, Jeanne Guyon found and lived in "the peace of God that passeth all understanding."[4] Today, in our hyperactive society and sometimes hyperactive religion, her teachings in this book could well bring a fresh oasis of peace and contentment in the midst of an often stormy and dry desert.

Harold J. Chadwick

[1] Philippians 3:10

[2] From the *Autobiography of Jeanne Guyon*

[3] In the Roman Catholic Church to which Jeanne belonged, there was usually a priest assigned as a *Confessor,* who would hear the person's sins and grant forgiveness, and one assigned as a *Director*, who would guide the person in the spiritual life.

[4] Philippians 4:7

BOOK ONE

EXPERIENCING UNION WITH
GOD THROUGH INNER PRAYER

"Walk before me and be thou perfect."
(Genesis 17:1)

PREFACE

This little treatise,[1] which was conceived in great simplicity, was not originally intended for publication. It was written for a few individuals who wanted to love God with all their heart. Many, however, because of the profit they received in reading the manuscript, wanted to obtain copies, and for this reason alone it was published.

It still retains its original simplicity. It contains no criticism of the various spiritual guidance of others.[2] On the contrary, it enforces the teachings that were received.

Everything here is submitted to the judgment of those who are learned[3] and experienced, with a request, however, that they not stop at the surface but enter into the main purpose of this book. That purpose is to *induce the whole world to love God, and to serve Him with comfort and success,* in a simple and easy manner. It is a manner that is especially adapted to those *little ones*[4] who are unqualified for learned and deep researches, but who earnestly *desire to be truly devoted to God.*

Unprejudiced readers will find a secret unction[5] hidden under the most common expressions. It is an unction that will inspire them to seek after the happiness that all should want to enjoy.

In declaring that perfection is easily attained, the word *facility*[6] is used, because God is indeed found with facility—[that is, He is easily found] *when we seek Him within ourselves.*

But some, perhaps, may [disagree and] advocate that passage in John's gospel, "Ye shall seek me, and shall not find me" (John 7:34, 36). This apparent difficulty, however, is removed by another passage, where He who cannot contradict Himself has said to all, "seek, and ye shall find."[7]

It is true, indeed, that those who seek God but are still unwilling to forsake their sins will not find Him— because they seek Him where He is not. Therefore, it is added, "Ye shall die in your sins."[8] But those who will take some trouble to seek God in their own heart, and sincerely forsake their sins so that they may draw near to Him, will certainly find Him.

[Living] a life of *piety*[9] appears so frightful[14] to many, and *prayer* so difficult to do,[10] that they are discouraged from taking a single step toward it. But [in the same way that] the anticipated[11] difficulty of an undertaking often causes [us to] despair of succeeding and [makes us] reluctant to start, its desirableness and the knowledge that it is easy to accomplish induce us to begin its pursuit with pleasure, and to pursue it with vigor. Therefore, the advantages and *facility* of this way [of praying] are presented for your consideration[12] in this treatise.

Once we are persuaded of the goodness of God toward His poor creatures, and of His desire to communicate Himself to us, we will not conceive impossible ideals,[13] nor so easily despair of obtaining the good that He so desires to bestow.

He that spared not His own Son, but delivered Him up for us all; how shall He not with Him also freely give us all things?" (Romans 8:32)

It takes only a little courage and perseverance. We have enough of both in our worldly concerns, but none at all in the one thing that is needful.[14]

If you think that God is not easily found in this way, do not change your mind because of my testimony. Just try it, and your own experience will convince you that the reality far exceeds all I have said about[15] it.

Beloved reader, study this little book with a sincere and impartial spirit, and with a humble mind—not with an inclination to criticize, and you will not fail to reap profit from it. It was written with a desire that you might *wholly devote yourself to God,* so receive it with a like desire. It has no other purpose than to invite the simple and the childlike to approach their Father, who delights in the humble confidence of His children, and who is greatly grieved at their distrust. Therefore, with a sincere desire for your salvation, seek nothing from the simple[16] method in this book[17] but the *love of God,* and you will assuredly obtain it.

Without setting up my opinions above those of others, I mean only to declare with sincerity from my own experience and the experience of others, the happy effects produced by following after the Lord in this simple manner.

Since this treatise was intended only to instruct in prayer, nothing is said of many things that I esteem, because they do not immediately relate to the main subject. It is beyond a doubt, however, that nothing in this book will offend—*if* the book is read in the spirit with which it was written. And it is still more certain, that those who earnestly try this simple way of prayer, will find I have written the truth.

It is You alone, O holy Jesus, who loves simplicity and innocence, "and whose delight is to dwell with the children of men,"[18] with those who are, indeed, willing to become "little children."[19]

It is You alone who can render this little work of any value, by imprinting it on the heart, and leading those who read it to seek You within themselves. [In that place] where You repose as in the manger, waiting to receive proofs of their love, and to give them testimony of Yours. They lose these advantages by their own fault.

But it belongs to You, O child Almighty!, uncreated Love!, silent and all-containing Word!, to make Yourself loved, enjoyed, and understood. You can do it; and I know You will do it by this little work, which belongs entirely to You, proceeds wholly from You, and tends[25] only toward You!

[1] *treatise:* a systematic, usually extensive written discourse on a subject.

[2] Madame Guyon is undoubtedly speaking of the teachings of the various Directors that were assigned to oversee her spiritual development over the years. It was the business of the Director to give religious counsel, especially in the beginning of someone's religious life. Sometimes the office of *Director* and the office of *Confessor* were vested in the same person, but usually they were different clerics.

[3] *learned:* possessing or demonstrating profound, often systematic knowledge; directed towards scholars (a *learned* treatise).

[4] *little ones:* a term of endearment for those who are babes in Christ.

[5] Unction: (1) the act of anointing as part of a religious, ceremonial, or healing ritual; (2) an ointment or oil; a salve; (3) something that serves to sooth; a balm.

[6] *facility:* ease in moving, acting, or doing.

[7] Matthew 7:7

[8] John 8:21, 24

[9] *piety:* the state or quality of being pious, especially: (a) religious devotion and reverence to God; (b) devotion and reverence to parents and family: *filial piety.*

[10] *frightful:* probably used in the sense of excessive, extreme; disagreeable, distressing.

[11] Original word: *attain*

[12] Original word: *apprehended*

[13] Original words: *set forth*

[14] Original words: *create ideal monsters*

[15] Luke 10:42

[16] Original words: *my representations of*

[17] Original word: *unpretending*

[18] Original words: *here proposed*

[19] Proverbs 8:31, KJV, reads: *Rejoicing in the habitable part of his earth; and my delights were with the sons of men.* No matching verse was found anywhere in any current Bible version.

[20] Matthew 18:3

[21] *tends:* to move in a certain direction.

1

THE PRAYER OF THE HEART

Introduction. All are called to prayer, and by the aid of ordinary grace may put up the prayer of the heart, which is the great means of [working out our] salvation, and which can be offered at all times, and by the most uninstructed. [Please read endnote[1]]

Everyone is capable of prayer, and it is a dreadful mistake[2] that almost everyone has[3] conceived the idea that they are not called to prayer. We are all called to prayer, just as we are all called to salvation.

Prayer is simply the act of applying your heart to God, and internally expressing love [to Him].[4] The apostle Paul[5] has instructed[6] us to "pray without ceasing,"[7] and our Lord directs us to "watch and pray."[8] Everyone may pray, therefore, and everyone should practice prayer.

I grant that few people meditate,[9] for few people are capable of doing it.[10] Therefore, meditative prayer is not the prayer that God requires of those who are thirsty for salvation, nor the manner of prayer that I recommend.

EVERYONE SHOULD PRAY

Everyone should pray—you should live by prayer, as you should live by love. "I counsel thee to buy of me gold tried in the fire, that thou mayest be rich."[11] This [gold] is very easily obtained, much more easily than you can imagine.[12]

All you who are thirsty, come to the living waters, and do not waste your precious moments in hewing out cisterns that can hold no water.[13] All you who are famished and find nothing to satisfy you, come and you will be filled. All you poor afflicted ones, bending beneath your load of wretchedness and pain, come and you will be consoled! All you who are sick, come to your Physician, and do not be afraid to approach Him because you are filled with diseases—show them [to Him], and you will be healed!

Children, draw near to your Father, and He will embrace you in the arms of love! Come you poor, stray, wandering sheep, return to your Shepherd! Come you sinners to your Savior! Come you dull, ignorant, and illiterate[14]—you who think you are the most incapable of prayer! You are uniquely[15] called and adapted to prayer[16]. Let everyone without exception come, for Jesus Christ has called everyone.

Those who are without a heart, however, are excused, for there must be a heart before there can be love. But who is without a heart? So come, then, and learn here how to give your heart to God.[17]

Everyone who desires to pray may easily pray, for the ordinary graces and gifts of the Holy Spirit that are common to everyone will enable you to do so.

PRAYER IS KEY TO PERFECTION

Prayer is the key to perfection, and to the sovereign good [received from God]. It is the means of delivering us from every vice, and obtaining us every virtue—for the one great means of becoming perfect is to walk in the presence of God. He Himself said, "Walk before Me, and be thou perfect."[18] It is by prayer alone that we are brought into His presence, and kept in it without interruption.

You must, then, learn a method[19] of prayer that may be exercised at all times, that does not interfere with[20] outward activities,[21] and that may be equally practiced by princes, kings, prelates, priests, magistrates, soldiers, tradesmen, laborers, children, men, women, sick people—by everyone. Such a prayer is not a prayer of the head, but of the heart.

It is not a prayer of the understanding alone, for the mind is so limited in its operations that it can have but one object at a time. This is a prayer of the heart, which is not interrupted by the activities of the mind.[22] Nothing can interrupt this prayer but unsettled[23] affections. Once we have enjoyed God and the sweetness of His love, however, we will find it impossible to enjoy anything[24] but Him.

PRESENCE OF GOD EASILY OBTAINED

Nothing is so easily obtained as the possession and enjoyment of [the presence of] God.[25] He is more attentive[26] [or *near*] to us than we are to ourselves. He desires more to give Himself to us than we desire to

11

possess Him. We only need to know how to seek Him, and the way [to do it] is easier and more natural to us than breathing.

Even if you think you are dull and fit for nothing,[27] by prayer you may live on God Himself with less difficulty or interruption than you live on the life-sustaining[28] air. Will it not be highly sinful then to neglect prayer? But without doubt you will not, once you have learned the method [in this book], which is the easiest [method] in the world.

[1] All the summaries at the beginning of the chapters were found in a different edition of Madame Guyon's book than the one we revised, but were added to this one because they are well done and useful to following the chapter text. The original spelling and language that was used in them indicates that there were probably written by a British editor in the 1800s.

[2] Original word: *misfortune*

[3] Original words: *all the world have*

[4] Original words: *nothing but the application of the heart to God, and the internal exercise of love.*

[5] Original: *St. Paul*

[6] Original word: *enjoined*

[7] 1 Thessalonians 5:17

[8] Mark 13:33

[9] Joshua 1:8, Psalm 1:1-3

[10] Original words: *meditation is attainable but by few, for few are capable of it*

[11] Revelation 3:18

[12] Original word: *conceive*

[13] John 7:37, Jeremiah 2:13

[14] Many people in Madam Guyon's day had no schooling and could not read.

[15] Original words: *more peculiarly*

[16] Original word: *thereto*

[17] Original words: *give this heart to God; and here learn how to make the donation*

[18] Genesis 17:1

[19] Original word: *species*

[20] Original word: *obstruct*

[21] Original word: *employments*

[22] Original words: *exercises of reason*

[23] Original word: *disordered*

[24] Original words: *relish aught*

[25] See *The Practice of the Presence of God* by Brother Lawrence, Pure Gold Classics, Bridge-Logos Publishers.

[26] Original word: *present* — Madame Guyon probably used this word in its now obsolete meaning of *attentive*. It also has two archaic meanings of *readily available* and *immediate*, but neither seem to fit the context of her sentence.

[27] Original words: *Ah! ye who think yourselves so dull*

[28] Original word: *vital*

2

THE FIRST DEGREE[1] OF PRAYER: MEDITATION

First degree of prayer, practiced in two ways; one by reading and meditation, the other by meditation alone. Rules and methods of meditation. Remedies for its difficulties.

There are two ways of introducing your soul to prayer, which should be pursued for some time. One is *meditative reading,* and the other is *meditation.* [Though closely linked, these two are not the same.]

*[To do] m*editative reading, *choose [a passage of Scripture from the Bible], or some important practical or speculative truth [from a truly spiritual book], always preferring the practical [from the latter], and proceed in the following way. Whatever passage you have chosen, read only a small amount of it. [Then mentally chew on it], doing your best to taste and digest it—to get all the strong meat*[2] *and nourishment out of*

it.³ Do not go any further while any [spiritual] taste or flavor⁴ remains in the passage—[that is, while you are still getting something spiritual out of it]. Then take up your book again and do as before, seldom reading more than half a page at a time.

IT IS NOT HOW MUCH WE READ THAT BENEFITS US, BUT THE WAY WE READ IT.⁵

Those who read fast obtain no more advantage than a bee would by only skimming over the surface of the flower instead of penetrating into it and extracting its sweets. Such reading is for scholastic subjects rather than divine truths. To profit from [the Bible and] spiritual books, we must read as I have described. I am certain that if we use that method, our [meditative reading] will gradually develop in us the habit of praying, and will make us much more inclined to pray.⁶

Meditation, which is the other method, should be done during times that you set aside especially to meditate, not to read.⁷ I believe that the best way to meditate is as follows.

By faith come into the presence of God, then read [or bring to mind] some truth or Bible verse in which there is solid spiritual food.⁸ Now think quietly about it, not to reason it out but merely to focus your mind.⁹ You use the Bible verse to help you focus your mind so that you will begin to be aware of the presence of God within you, so do not concentrate on the verse itself or try to reason it out.¹⁰

GOD IS FOUND WITHIN YOU

Now by an active *faith in God in your soul,* eagerly [and expectantly] sink into yourself—[into your innermost being], preventing all your senses from

16

wandering about [by continuing to focus on your Bible verse]. Doing this will keep you from numerous distractions, remove your thoughts from external things, and draw you near to God.[11] For He is only to be found in your innermost center, which is the *Holy of Holies* in which He dwells.[12] He has even promised to come and make His abode with those who do His will.[13] St. Augustine blamed himself for the time he had lost in not having sought God in this manner of prayer from the beginning.

When you have fully withdrawn your thoughts into yourself,[14] you will sense within you the warm presence of God. When your senses are all gathered together[15] and withdrawn from the external[16] to the internal,[17] let your soul linger sweetly and silently on the Scripture verse you have read.[18] Do not try to reason out the truth in it, just let your soul feed on it.[19] Encourage and strengthen your will to do this by your love for God, rather than tiring your mind with constant study.[20] Now when your affections warmly sense the presence of God within you—which is a state that may appear difficult at first, but as I will soon show is easily attained, allow them to *rest lovingly* [upon the truth] and to *absorb* or *swallow* what they have tasted.[21]

For we may enjoy the flavor of delicious food when chewing it,[22] yet we will get no nourishment from the food if we do not stop chewing and swallow it. In the same way, if we try to stir up our affections even more when they are aroused, we extinguish the flame and our soul is deprived of its nourishment. We should, therefore, in a *restful state of love,*[23] full of respect and confidence, *swallow* the blessed [spiritual] food we have received. This method is highly effective, and will advance the soul more in a short time than any other [method] will in years.

FOCUS ALL YOUR THOUGHTS AND SENSES INWARD ON GOD'S PRESENCE

Now because our direct and principal exercise should be contemplating the presence of God within us, the most easy method of overcoming outward distractions is to gather all our senses and thoughts and focus them on His inward presence.[24] Concentrating directly upon the distractions only serves to arouse and increase them.[25] But by withdrawing ourselves inward by faith in the indwelling presence of God, we fight without conscious involvement a very successful and indirect war with them.

Beginners in this method of prayer should be careful about wandering from truth to truth, and from subject to subject. The right way to penetrate every divine truth, to enjoy it to its fullness, and to imprint it on the heart, is to dwell upon it while its flavor and nourishment continue.

OUR SOUL TENDS TO WANDER

Withdrawing inwardly is *difficult* in the beginning, because of the habit the soul has developed of always wandering from one worldly thing to another. But as you discipline your soul to focus inwardly, it becomes more accustomed to it, and then does it very easily. This easiness is partly from the force of the new habit, and partly because God, whose one will toward His creatures is to communicate Himself to them, imparts abundant grace. Added to those is the fact that experiencing the enjoyment of God's indwelling presence makes it very easy to return to it time and again.

[1] *Degree*: one of a series of steps in a process, course, or progression; a stage: *learned by degrees the simple and easy method of prayer.*

[2] Hebrews 5:14

[3] Original words: *to extract the essence and substance of it*

[4] Original words: *savor or relish*

[5] Mark 4:23-25

[6] Original words: *we should become gradually habituated to prayer by our reading, and more fully disposed for its exercise.*

[7] Original words: *is to be practised at an appropriated season, and not in the time of reading*

[8] Original words: *wherein there is substance*

[9] Original words: *pause gently thereon, not to employ the reason, but merely to fix the mind*

[10] Original words: *observing that the principal exercise should ever be the presence of God, and that the subject, therefore, should rather serve to stay the mind, than exercise it in reasoning.*

[11] Original words: *this serves to extricate us, in the first instance, from numerous distractions, to remove us far from external objects, and to bring us nigh to God, . . .*

[12] 1 Corinthians 6:19, Philippians 2:13

[13] John 14:23

[14] Original words: *entered into yourself*

[15] Original words: *the senses are all recollected*

[16] Original word: *circumference*

[17] Original word: *centre*

[18] Original words: *and the soul is sweetly and silently employed on the truths we have read,*

[19] Original words: *not in reasoning, but in feeding thereon*

[20] Original words: *and animating the will by affection, rather than fatiguing the understanding by study*

[21] Original words: *when, I say, the affections are in this state, (which, however difficult it may appear at first, is, as I shall hereafter show, easily attainable,) we must allow them sweetly to repose, and, as it were, swallow what they have tasted.*

[22] Original words: *the finest viands in mastication*

[23] Original words: *repose of love*

[24] Original words: *But as I have said that our direct and principal exercise should consist in the contemplation of the Divine presence, we should be exceedingly diligent in recalling our dissipated senses, as the most easy method of overcoming distractions;*

[25] Original words: *irritate and augment them.*

3

THE METHOD OF PRAYER FOR THOSE WHO HAVE DIFFICULTY READING[1]

Method of meditative prayer for those who cannot read [or have difficulty reading]; applied to the Lord's Prayer and to some of the attributes of God. Transition from the first to the second degree of prayer. Those who cannot read books, [or who have difficulty reading], are not excluded from prayer because of that. The great book that teaches [us] all things, and that is written all over, inside and outside, is Jesus Christ Himself.

The method the above class of people should practice is as follows. First learn the fundamental truth that "the kingdom of God is within you,"[2] and that it must be searched for only there.

It is as much the duty of the clergy to instruct their church members[3] in prayer, as in the basic principles of Christianity.[4] It is true they tell them God's intended purpose for their lives[5]—[that they should be saved through Jesus Christ]. But they do not give them sufficient instructions on how they may obtain [the fullness of their salvation].[6]

BEGIN PRAYER WITH AN ACT OF ADORATION

[Since prayer is the easiest way], they should be taught to begin [prayer] with an act of profound adoration, eliminating any thoughts of themselves,[7] before God. They should then close their physical eyes and attempt to open the spiritual eyes of their soul. Now they should gather their thoughts inward, and by a lively faith in the presence of God within them, enter gently into His presence.[8] They should not allow their thoughts to wander around, but should keep them in control.[9]

REPEAT THE LORD'S PRAYER SLOWLY

Now they should repeat the Lord's prayer [slowly] in their native language.[10] [As they do], they should think a little about the meaning of the words, ["Our Father, who art in heaven"], and the infinite willingness of God, who dwells within them, to become truly "their Father." In this state, let them pour out their wants before Him. When they [softly] speak the name *Father,* they should remain a few moments in a reverential silence, waiting to have the will of their heavenly Father made known to them.

SPEAK QUIET WORDS OF LOVE

Again, Christians [praying in this manner] should see themselves in the condition[11] of feeble children, soiled and sorely bruised by repeated falls, destitute of strength to stand, or of power to cleanse themselves. They should humbly lay their unhappy condition[12] open to their Father's view. Occasionally, they should speak a [quiet] word or two of love and grief, and then again sink into silence before Him. Then, continuing the Lord's prayer, let them beseech the King of Glory to reign in them, abandoning themselves to God so He may do it, and acknowledging His right to rule over them.

HUMBLY BESEECH GOD TO ACCOMPLISH HIS WILL IN YOU

If they feel a sense of peace and quiet, they should not continue the words of the prayer so long as this sensation remains. When it subsides, they should go on with the second petition, *"Thy will be done on earth as it is in heaven!"* By these words they should humbly beseech God to accomplish in them, and by them, all His will. And they should surrender their hearts and freedom into His hands, to do with it as He pleases. When they learn that their will should be used in loving, they will desire to love, and will beseech God for His LOVE. But all this will [gradually] take place sweetly and peacefully, as will the rest of the prayer, in which the clergy should instruct them.

But they should not burden[13] themselves with frequent repetitions of set forms or memorized prayers, for the Lord's prayer used as I have just described will produce abundant fruit.

At other times, they may place themselves as sheep before their Shepherd, looking up to Him for their true food, [and saying something like], "O divine Shepherd, You feed Your flock with Yourself, and are indeed our daily bread." They may also present to Him the necessities of their families. Let all be done, however, from this principal and one great view of faith—God is within them.

HAVE FAITH IN GOD'S PRESENCE WITHIN YOU

All our imaginations of God amount to nothing—a lively faith in His presence [within us] is sufficient.[14] We must not form any image of the Deity, though we may of Jesus Christ, seeing Him in His birth, or His crucifixion, or in some other state or mystery, provided the soul always seeks Him in its own center.

On other occasions, we may look to Him as a Physician, and present for His healing virtue all our illnesses. But always without anxiety,[15] and with pauses from time to time so that the silence, being mingled with action, may be gradually extended and our own effort lessened. By continually yielding to God's operations, there will come a time when He gains sovereign control[16] [of your soul], as shall be explained later.

WHEN GOD GRANTS THE SENSE OF HIS DIVINE PRESENCE

When the [sense of the] divine presence is granted to us, and we gradually begin to [experience and] enjoy silence and peacefulness, *this experimental enjoyment of the presence of God* will introduce our soul into the second degree of prayer. By proceeding in the manner I have described, this second degree can be achieved as well by the illiterate as by the learned. Indeed, some privileged souls are favored with it even from the beginning.

[1] Original title: *The Method of Prayer for Those Who Cannot Read* — During Madame Guyon's time, only the financially privileged were given an education, and many of the middle-class citizens, and most of the poor, could barely read or not read at all. This was especially true of women, who were often shunted aside in matters of education. There were also, of course, many people with weak eyes who could not see to read and many blind people. Seldom were any of these given an education, because it was felt it would be of no use to them. Although this chapter in Madame Guyon's book does not apply much today, it contains some excellent information and so is included in this revised version. It is also included so that those who can read will know how to teach this short and easy method of prayer to those who cannot, or who can only read with difficulty.

[2] Luke 17:21

[3] Original word: *parishioners*

[4] Original words: *their catechism;* Hebrews 6:1-2

[5] Original words: *the end of their creation*

[6] Philippians 1:6, 2:12-13

[7] Original words: *and annihilation*

[8] Original words: *they should then collect themselves inwardly, and by a lively faith in God, as dwelling within them, pierce into the divine presence;*

[9] Original words: *senses to wander abroad, but holding them as much as may be in subjection.*

[10] "in their native language" may have related to the fact that France, where Madame Guyon lived, was surrounded by many other nations, whose citizens spoke a language other than French—or it might have to do

with people from other nations who had settled in France. The citizens of surrounding countries were often more poorly educated than those in France.

[11] Original words: *beholding the state*

[12] Original words: *deplorable situation*

[13] Original word: *burthen*

[14] Ephesians 3:17

[15] Original word: *perturbation*

[16] Original words: *complete ascendancy*

4

THE PRAYER OF SIMPLICITY

Second degree of prayer, called here, "The prayer of simplicity." At what time we reach it. How to offer and continue it. Requirements to offering it acceptably

Some call the second degree [or stage] of prayer, contemplation, or the prayer of faith and stillness, and others call it the prayer of simplicity. I will use this latter name,[1] because this prayer method involves more than just pure contemplation, which is a more advanced state than I am dealing with now. [2]

When your soul has been for some time exercised in the way I have discussed, it gradually finds that it is able[3] to approach God with ease,[4] that drawing your thoughts inward is much less difficult,[5] and that prayer becomes easy, sweet, and delightful. Your soul [increasingly] recognizes that this is the true way of finding God, and feels that "His name is as ointment poured forth."[6] The method must now be altered, however, and what I describe must be pursued with courage and faithfulness, without being disturbed by the difficulties we may encounter along the way.

REMAIN SILENT IN GOD'S PRESENCE

First, as soon as the soul by faith places itself in the presence of God, and becomes focused upon[7] Him, let it remain that way for a little time in respectful silence.

If at the beginning, however, when you are starting to exercise your faith, your souls feels even a small pleasing sense of the Divine presence, let it remain there without being concerned about a subject [for prayer]. Do not go any further, but carefully cherish this sensation while it continues. When it begins to lessen, it may stir up some tender emotion in you and immediately return your soul to a feeling of sweet peace. If it does, let your soul remain there quietly.[8] The fire must be gently fanned, but as soon as it is kindled we must stop our efforts, lest we put it out by our activity.

PRAY TO PLEASE GOD

I warmly recommend that you never finish prayer without remaining for a while afterward in a respectful silence. It is also very important for the soul to go to prayer with courage, and to bring with it a pure and disinterested[9] love that seeks nothing from God but to please Him and to do His will. For servants who only work in proportion to their wages, are unworthy of any payment.[10] Pray, therefore, not because you desire spiritual delights, but just to please God.[11] This will keep your spirit tranquil in dry seasons as well as in seasons of comfort,[12] and prevent your being surprised at what appears to be the rejection[13] or absence of God.

[1] Original word: *appellation*

[2] Original words: *being more than just that of contemplation, which implies a more advanced state than that I am now treating of.*

[3] Original word: *enabled*

[4] Original word: *facility*

[5] Original words: *recollection is attended with much less difficulty*

[6] Song of Songs 1:3

[7] Original words: *recollected before*

[8] Original words: *When it abates, it may excite the will by some tender affection; and if, by the first moving thereof, it finds itself reinstated in sweet peace, let it there remain;*

[9] free of self-interest

[10] Original words: *for a servant who only proportions his diligence to his hope of reward, is unworthy of any recompense.*

[11] Original words: *Go then to prayer, not desiring to enjoy spiritual delights, but to be just as it pleases God;*

[12] Original words: *this will preserve your spirit tranquil in aridities as well as in consolation*

[13] Original words: *apparent repulses*

5

SURVIVE DRY SEASONS THROUGH LOVE[1]

On various matters occurring in or belonging to the degree of prayer, that is to say—on [periods of] dryness, which are caused by deprivation of the sensible presence of God for an admirable end, and which is to be met by acts of solid and peaceful virtue of mind and soul. Advantages of this course.

Although God has no other desire than to impart Himself to the loving soul that seeks Him, He often conceals Himself from it so that it may be aroused from laziness, and driven to seek Him with faithfulness and love. But He always rewards the faithfulness of His beloved with [an outpouring of] abundant goodness![2] And often the withdrawing of the sense of His presence is followed by the caress of [His] love![3]

WAIT REVERENTLY AND SILENTLY FOR THE SENSE OF GOD'S PRESENCE

During such times we are apt to believe that it proves our faithfulness, and demonstrates[4] a greater intensity of love, if we seek Him by exerting our own strength and activity. Or that so doing will persuade Him to return [the sense of] His presence to us more quickly.[5] No, dear soul, believe me, this is not the best way in this stage[6] of prayer. You must await the return of your Beloved with patient love, with self-denial and humility,[7] with repeated whisperings of a strong but undisturbed love,[8] and with deep and reverent silence.[9]

Only in this way can you demonstrate [to God] that it is only Him and His good pleasure that you seek, and not any selfish delights in the feelings you get in loving Him.[10] That is why it is written: "Be not impatient in the time of dryness and obscurity; suffer the suspensions and delays of the consolations of God; cleave unto Him, and wait upon Him patiently, that thy life may increase and be renewed."[11]

BE PATIENT IN PRAYER

Be patient in prayer, and throughout your whole lifetime simply wait for the return[12] of your Beloved in a spirit of humility, abandonment, contentment, and resignation. [This is a] most excellent prayer! Especially when it is mixed together with sighs of mournful[13] love [that express how you miss the sense of His presence]! This conduct indeed is most pleasing to the heart of God, and will, above all others, compel His return [to you].

[1] Original title: *Aridities to Be Borne in Love*

[2] Original words: *with what abundant goodness does He recompense the faithfulness of His beloved!*

[3] Original words: *And how often are these apparent withdrawings of Himself succeeded by the caresses of love!*

[4] Original word: *evinces*

[5] Original words: *induce Him the more speedily to revisit us.*

[6] Original word: *degree*

[7] Original words: *self-abasement and humiliation*

[8] Original words: *the reiterated breathings of an ardent but peaceful affection*

[9] Original words: *and with silence full of veneration*

[10] Original words: *of your own sensations in loving Him.*

[11] This is from Ecclesiasticus 2:2-3, in the Apocrypha, which most Protestant Bibles do not contain. The Bible version is unknown. A common version reads: "Humble thy heart, and endure: incline thy ear, and receive the words of understanding: and make not haste in the time of clouds. Wait on God with patience: join thyself to God, and endure, that thy life may be increased in the latter end."

[12] Original words: *do nothing else than wait the return*

[13] Original word: *plaintive*

6

THE IMPORTANCE OF SELF-ABANDONMENT

On the abandonment of self to God, its fruit, and its irrevocableness. Its nature, [and] that God requires it. Its practice.

Now we must begin to *abandon* and give up our whole existence to God. [We must do this] from the strong and positive conviction that what happens[1] every moment comes from His immediate will and permission, and is exactly what[2] our [spiritual] condition needs.[3] This conviction will make us content with everything,[4] and make us see[5] all that happens [to us] from God's side and not from our own.[6]

ABANDON YOURSELF TO GOD

But, dearly beloved, if you sincerely wish to[7] give yourself up to God, I urge[8] you that after having done so[9] you do not take yourself back again. Remember,

35

once a gift is presented it is no longer at the disposal of the giver.

Abandonment is a matter of the greatest importance in our progress. It is the key to the inner court. Those who know truly how to abandon themselves will soon become perfect. We must, therefore, continue steadfast and immovable in our abandonment,[10] without listening to the voice of natural reason. Great faith produces great abandonment. We must put ourselves into God's keeping,[11] "hoping against hope."[12] *Abandonment* is the casting off of all selfish care, that we may be completely[13] at God's[14] disposal. All Christians are exhorted to abandonment, for it is said to all:

Take no thought for the morrow, for your Heavenly Father knoweth that ye have need of all these things.[15]

"In all thy ways acknowledge Him, and He shall direct thy paths.[16]

Commit thy works unto the LORD, and thy thoughts shall be established."[17]

"Commit thy way unto the LORD; trust also in Him; and He shall bring it to pass."[18]

With respect to both external and internal things, our abandonment[19] should be an absolute giving up of all our concerns into the hands of God, forgetting ourselves and thinking only of Him. By doing this, the heart will remain always disengaged [from all concerns], free, and at peace.

CONTINUALLY SURRENDER YOUR WILL TO GOD'S WILL

We practice this by continually surrendering our own will to the will of God, and renouncing every private inclination as soon as it arises, however good it may appear [to be]. We must become indifferent with respect to ourselves, only will what God has willed [for us] from all eternity, and resign ourselves in all things, whether for soul or body, for time or eternity. We must also forget the past, leave the future to Providence, devote the present to God, and be satisfied with the present moment. [Whatever this moment brings, it also] brings with it God's eternal order in respect to us, and is as infallible a declaration of His will as it is unavoidable and common to all.[20] Further, we must attribute nothing that befalls us as being from people. Instead, seeing everything as being in God, we must look upon everything, except our sins, as *infallibly*[21] coming from Him.[22]

Surrender yourself, therefore, to be led and disposed of just as God pleases, with respect both to your outward and inward state.[23]

[1] Original words: *the occurrences of*

[2] Original words: *are just such as*

[3] Original words: *state requires*

[4] Not that I speak in regard to need, for I have learned in whatever state I am, to be content (Philippians 4:11).

[5] Original words: *cause us to regard*

[6] Original words: *not from the side of the creature, but from that of God*

[7] Original words: *whoever you are who*

[8] Original word: *conjure* (Whatever Madame Guyon meant by this word, the word certainly does not mean the same thing today, so undoubtedly it meant something different in her day, or the French word she used was translated into English incorrectly.)

[9] Original words: *having once made the donation*

[10] Original words: *immoveable therein*

[11] Original words: *confide in God*

[12] A paraphrase of Romans 4:18.

[13] Original word: *altogether*

[14] Original word: *the divine*

[15] Reversal of parts of Matthew 6:32 and 34.

[16] Proverbs 3:6

[17] Proverbs 16:3

[18] Psalm 37:5

[19] Original words: *Our abandonment, then, should be, both in respect to external and internal things,*

[20] There hath no temptation taken you but such as is common to man: but God is faithful, who will not suffer you to be tempted above that ye are able; but will with

the temptation also make a way to escape, that ye may be able to bear it. (1 Corinthians 10:13)

[21] By *infallibly*, Madame Guyon undoubtedly means "without error and without possibility of failing in whatever God intends it to accomplish in our lives.

[22] Original paragraph: *It is practised by continually losing our own will in the will of God; renouncing every private inclination as soon as it arises, however good it may appear, that we may stand in indifference with respect to ourselves, and only will what God has willed from all eternity; resigning ourselves in all things, whether for soul or body, for time or eternity; forgetting the past, leaving the future to Providence, and devoting the present to God; satisfied with the present moment, which brings with it God's eternal order in reference to us, and is as infallible a declaration of his will, as it is inevitable and common to all; attributing nothing that befalls us to the creature, but regarding all things in God, and looking upon all, excepting only our sins, as infallibly proceeding from Him.*

[23] condition and circumstances

7

CONSOLATION IN SUFFERING[1]

On suffering: that it should be accepted from the hand of God. Its use and profit. Its practice.

Be patient under all the sufferings God sends you. If your love to Him is pure, you will not seek Him less on Calvary than on Tabor.[2] Surely He should be as much loved on one as on the other, [especially] since it was on Calvary that He made the greatest display of [His] love.

[Do not] be not like those who give themselves to Him at one season, only to withdraw from Him at another. They give themselves [to Him] only to be caressed, and pull[3] themselves back again when they are crucified—or turn to others to be consoled.[4]

LOVE THE CROSS

No, beloved souls, you will not find consolation in anything[5] but in the love of the cross, and in total abandonment. Whoever is not devoted to the cross, is

41

not devoted to the things that are of God.[6] It is impossible to love God without loving the cross, and a heart devoted to[7] [the work of] the cross, finds the bitterest things to be sweet. "To the hungry soul every bitter thing is sweet,"[8] because it finds itself hungering for God in the same degree or measure as it hungers for the cross.[9] God gives us the cross, and the cross gives us God.

We may be certain there is internal [spiritual] progress,[10] when there is progress in the work[11] of the cross. Abandonment and the cross go hand in hand.[12]

GIVE SUFFERING TO GOD AS A SACRIFICE

As soon as anything is presented in the form of suffering, and you feel an extreme dislike[13] [for it, and want to turn away from it], resign yourself [and the suffering] immediately to God—give yourself [and the suffering] up to Him in sacrifice. You will then find that when the cross arrives, it will not be much of a burden,[14] because you have yourself desired it, [and have submitted yourself to it]. This, however, does not prevent you from feeling its weight, as some have imagined, for when we do not feel the cross, we do not suffer. A sensitiveness[15] to suffering is one of the principal parts of suffering itself. Jesus Christ Himself chose to endure its maximum severity.[16] Often we bear the cross in weakness, and at other times in strength, but both should be alike to us in the will of God.

[1] Original title: *Suffering – A Source of Consolation*

[2] Some Bible scholars have felt that Tabor was the mountain on which Jesus was transfigured (Luke 9:28-36), but many other Bible scholars have said that this is highly improbable. *Unger's Bible Dictionary* states, "In the time of [Jesus] the summit is said to have been crowned by a fortified town, the ruins of which are present there now (1 Chronicles 6:77). It is difficult to see how such a scene as that of [Jesus'] transfiguration could have taken place there, and the New Testament clearly points to some part of Hermon as the place [where the transfiguration occurred]."

[3] Original word: *wrest*

[4] Original words: *at least turn for consolation to the creature.*

[5] Original word: *aught*

[6] Original words: *who savoreth not the cross, savoreth not the things that be of God.* (See Matthew 16:23.)

[7] Original words: *that savors*

[8] Proverbs 27:7

[9] Original words: *proportion as it is hungering* "For with the same measure that you use, it will be measured back to you" (Luke 6:38b, NKJV)

[10] Original words: *an internal advancement*

[11] Original word: *way*

[12] Original words: *hand in hand together*

[13] Original words: *a repugnance*

[14] Original words: *so very burthensome*

[15] Original word: sensibility

[16] Original words: *utmost rigors* (See Luke 24:26 and Hebrews 12:2.)

8

REVELATION OF MYSTERIES[1]

On mysteries; God gives them in this state in reality. We must let Him bestow or withhold as seems good to Him, with a loving regard to His will.

Some may object[2] that by this method[3] we will have no mysteries revealed to us.[4] This is not only far from being the case, [5] it is the special[6] means of imparting them to the soul. Jesus Christ to whom we are abandoned, whom we follow as the Way, whom we hear as the Truth, and who animates us as the Life,[7] imprints Himself on our soul and impresses there the characters of His different states. To bear all the states of Jesus Christ is a much greater thing than merely to meditate about them. The apostle Paul[8] bore in his body the states of Jesus Christ. He said, "I bear in my body the marks of the Lord Jesus.[9] He does not, however, say that he meditated on them[10]—[he simply bore them].

Thankfully accept whatever appears to be God's will

In this condition of abandonment, Jesus Christ frequently communicates some special manifestations or revelations of His states. These we should thankfully accept, and give ourselves over to whatever appears to be His will. We should receive equally whatever state or circumstances He sends us. In truth, we have no other choice but to ardently reach out for Him, dwell ever with Him, and sink into nothingness before Him, So we should accept all His gifts without selecting just the ones we want. No matter whether darkness or illumination, productivity or barrenness, weakness or strength, sweetness or bitterness, temptations, distractions, pain, weariness, or uncertainty. None of these should for one moment slow down our progress.[11]

Whoever loves God loves all that belongs to God

God keeps some people absorbed for years in meditating and enjoying a single mystery, which draws their soul inward because of their uncomplicated examination or meditation of it.[12] Let those be faithful to it. But as soon as God is pleased to withdraw this meditation[13] from your[14] soul, freely yield to the withdrawal.[15] Some are very concerned about[16] their inability to meditate on certain mysteries. But there is no reason for such concern,[17] since love for God contains within itself every kind of devotion.[18] Therefore, whoever is calmly united to God alone[19] [by love], is, indeed, most wonderfully and adequately devoted to every divine mystery.[20] [For] whoever loves God loves all that belongs[21] to Him.

[1] Original title: *On Mysteries*

[2] Original words: *It will be objected*

[3] The short and very easy method of prayer that Madame Guyon is teaching.

[4] Original words: *imprinted on our minds.*

[5] Original words: *but so far is this from being the case, that*

[6] Original word: *peculiar*

[7] John 14:6

[8] Original words: *St. Paul*

[9] Galatians 6:17

[10] Original words: *reasoned thereon*

[11] Original paragraph: *In this state of abandonment Jesus Christ frequently communicates some peculiar views, or revelations of his states: these we should thankfully accept, and dispose ourselves for what appears to be his will; receiving equally whatever frame He may bestow, and having no other choice, but that of ardently reaching after Him, of dwelling ever with Him, and of sinking into nothingness before Him, and accepting indiscriminately all his gifts, whether darkness or illumination, fecundity or barrenness, weakness or strength, sweetness or bitterness, temptations, distractions, pain, weariness, or uncertainty; and none of all these should, for one moment, retard our course.*

[12] Original sentence: *God engages some, for whole years, in the contemplation and enjoyment of a single mystery; the simple view or contemplation of which recollects the soul;*

[13] Original word: *view*

[14] Original word: *the*

[15] Original word: *deprivation* [loss]

[16] Original words: *uneasy at*

[17] Original words: *but without reason,*

[18] Original words: *since an affectionate attachment to God includes in itself every species of devotion,*

[19] One with God in Christ without any emotional agitation or concern.

[20] Original words: *and whoever is calmly united to God alone, is, indeed, most excellently and effectually applied to every divine mystery.*

[21] Original word: *appertains*

9

ACQUIRING VIRTUE[1]

On virtue. All virtues come with God and are solidly and deeply implanted in the soul in this degree of the prayer of the heart. This takes place without difficulty.

It is through this method[2] that we acquire virtue[3] — [moral excellence, righteousness, goodness]—with ease and certainty, for since God is the source of everything good,[4] we receive it when we possess [or contain] Him.[5] The amount of God that we contain[6] is the same amount of divine virtue[7] that we receive.[8] For all virtue is like[9] a mask, an outside appearance that is as changeable[10] as our garments if it is not given[11] from within. [If it is], then, indeed, it is genuine, essential, and permanent: "The King's daughter is all glorious within," says David.[12] Souls in this state,[13] above all others, practice virtue in the highest[14] degree, though they do not refer or call attention[15] to any particular virtue. God, to whom they are united, leads them into the most extensive practice of it. He is exceedingly jealous over them,[16] and does not permit them to find the smallest pleasure[17] [in anything but Himself].

AS LOVE FOR GOD INCREASES, LOVE FOR *SELF* DECREASES

What a hungering for sufferings those souls have, who so glow with divine love! They would throw themselves into excessive self-discipline and self-denial, if [God] permitted them to pursue their own desires![18] They think of nothing except[19] how they may please their Beloved, and they [often] begin to neglect and forget themselves. As their love for God increases, so does dislike of their old nature and disinterest in themselves.[20]

ONLY LOVE IS REQUIRED

O if this simple method were only practiced, how easily would the whole Church of God be reformed, for it is a way so suited to all, to the dull and ignorant as well as to the most learned. Only LOVE is required: "Love," says St. Augustine, "and then do what you please." For when we truly love, we cannot even[21] will to do anything that might offend the object of our love.

[1] Original title: *On Virtue*

[2] Original words: *It is thus*

[3] *virtue:* moral excellence and righteousness; goodness.

[4] Luke 18:19

[5] Original words: *for as God is the principle of all virtue, we inherit all in the possession of Himself;*

[6] Ephesians 3:19

[7] Hebrews 12:10, 1 Peter 1:4

[8] Original words: *in proportion as we approach toward His possession, in like proportion do we receive the most eminent virtues.*

[9] Original words: *but as*

[10] Original word: *mutable*

[11] Original word: *bestowed*

[12] Psalm 45:13

[13] Original words: *These souls,*

[14] Original word: *most eminent*

[15] Original words: *advert*

[16] Exodus 34:14, Deuteronomy 4:24 (Or do you think that the Scripture says in vain, "The Spirit who dwells in us yearns jealously"? James 4:5, NKJV)

[17] Original words: *permits them not the least pleasure.*

[18] Original words: *How would they precipitate themselves into excessive austerities, were they permitted to pursue their own inclinations!*

[19] Original words: *nought save*

[20] Original words: *self-detestation and disregard of the creature.*

[21] Original words: *have so much as a.*

10

CONTROL OF THE FLESH MUST BE FROM WITHIN[1]

On mortification: that it is never perfect when it is solely exterior. But it must be accomplished by dwelling upon God within. Which, however, does not dispense with its outward practice to some degree. Hence, a sound conversion.

It is next to impossible to develop control[2] of the senses and passions in any other way [than by this short and easy method of prayer].[3]

FOCUSING ON THE SENSES STRENGTHENS THEM

The reason is obvious. The soul gives strength[4] and energy to the senses, and the senses increase[5] and stimulate the passions. A dead body has neither sensations nor passions, because its connection with the soul is dissolved. All attempts to just correct the exterior push the soul even further outward into what it is already warmly and eagerly doing.[6] Its ability to discipline itself is thereby weakened and broken up.[7] This happens because by focusing its attention upon severe bodily discipline and other externals, it actually energizes those very senses it is trying to subdue.[8] For the senses have no other source from which to get their strength than the soul's attention to them, and the amount of their life and activity is in direct proportion to the amount of attention the soul gives them.[9] The energized senses then stir up and excite the passions instead of suppressing and subduing them.[10] Severe bodily discipline may weaken the body [and its passions], but for the reasons just mentioned it can never weaken the senses or lessen their activity.[11]

TO OVERCOME THE SENSES, DRAW YOUR SOUL INWARD

The only way to overcome the senses is to draw the soul completely inward to an awareness of the presence of the indwelling God.[12] If the soul directs all its strength and energy within, this simple act separates it from the senses. By focusing its attention inward, it weakens the senses, and is nearer to the inward awareness of God the more it is separated from awareness of self—[that is, becomes less aware of body and senses].[13] That is why those in whom the attraction of grace—[the drawing inward to the Source of all grace]—is very powerful, are [sometimes] completely without energy and strength and are even subject to fainting.[14]

I do not mean by this to discourage physical self-denial, for it should always accompany prayer, in keeping with[15] the strength and state of the person, or as obedience demands. But physical self-denial should not be our principal exercise, nor should we prescribe severe disciplines for ourselves.[16] If we simply follow the internal attractions of grace and become occupied with God's presence, without thinking particularly on physical self-denial, God will enable us to perform every variety of it.[17] To those who abide faithful to their abandonment to Him, He gives no relaxation until He has subdued everything in them that still needs to be disciplined.[18]

CONTINUE STEADFAST IN GIVING ALL YOUR ATTENTION TO GOD

Therefore we have only to continue steadfast in giving all our attention to God, and all things will be perfectly done. Not every one is capable of physical self-denial, but all are capable of this. In disciplining the[19] eye and ear, which continually supply the busy imagination with new subjects, there is little danger of falling into excess.[20] But God will teach us this also, and we have only to follow His Spirit.

The soul has a double advantage by proceeding in this way: in withdrawing from outward objects it constantly draws nearer to God, and the nearer it draws to Him the further it is removed from sin. In addition, it receives the sustaining and preserving power and righteousness[21] that is known by only a few.[22] Thus its conversion [and salvation] become firmly established as a matter of habit.[23]

[1] Original title: *Mortification Must Be Interiour*

[2] Original word: *mortification* — This is the discipline of the body and the appetites by self-denial or self-inflicted privation.

[3] Original sentence: *I say further, that, in any other way, it is next to impossible to acquire a perfect mortification of the sense and passions.*

[4] Original word: *vigor*

[5] Original word: *raise*

[6] Original sentence: *All endeavors merely to rectify the exterior impel the soul yet farther outward into that about which it is so warmly and zealously engaged.*

[7] Original sentence: *Its powers are diffused and scattered abroad;*

[8] Original sentence: *for, its whole attention being immediately directed to austerities and other externals, it thus invigorates those very senses it is aiming to subdue.*

[9] Original sentence: *For the senses have no other spring whence to derive their vigor than the application of the soul to themselves, the degree of their life and activity being proportioned to the degree of attention which the soul bestows upon them.*

[10] Original sentence: *This life of the senses stirs up and provokes the passions, instead of suppressing or subduing them;*

[11] Original sentence: *austerities may indeed enfeeble the body, but for the reasons just mentioned, can never take off the keenness of the senses, nor lessen their activity.*

[12] Original sentence: *The only method of effecting this,*

is inward recollection, by which the soul is turned wholly and altogether inward, to possess a present God.

[13] Original sentence: *and, employing all its powers internally, it renders them faint; and the nearer it draws to God, the farther is it separated from self*

[14] Original sentence: *Hence it is, that those in whom the attractions of grace are very powerful, find the outward man altogether weak and feeble, and even liable to faintings.*

[15] Original words: *according to*

[16] Original sentence: *But I say, that mortification should not be our principal exercise; nor should we prescribe to ourselves such and such austerities.*

[17] Original sentence: *but simply following the internal attractions of grace, and being occupied with the divine presence, without thinking particularly on mortification, God will enable us to perform every species of it.*

[18] And the very God of peace sanctify you wholly; and I pray God your whole spirit and soul and body be preserved blameless unto the coming of our Lord Jesus Christ. Faithful is He that calleth you, who also will do it. (1 Thessalonians 5:23-24)

[19] Original words: *In the mortification of*

[20] Matthew 5:28-29

[21] Original word: *virtue*

[22] God hath from the beginning chosen you to salvation through sanctification of the Spirit and belief of the truth. (2 Thessalonians 2:13)

[23] Original paragraph: *The soul has a double advantage by proceeding thus; in withdrawing from outward*

objects it constantly draws nearer to God; and besides the secret sustaining and preserving power and virtue which it receives, it is farther removed from sin the nearer it comes to Him; so that its conversion becomes firmly established as a matter of habit.

11

PERFECT CONVERSION[1]

On the perfect conversion that is the result of this kind of prayer, and how it is accomplished. Two of its aids: the drawing of God, and the tendency of the soul to its center. Its practice.

> Turn ye unto *Him from* whom the
> children of Israel have deeply revolted.
> (Isaiah 31:6)

Conversion is nothing more than turning from yourself[2] in order to return to God.[3]

Conversion, however, no matter how good and essential it is to salvation,[4] is not perfect when it consists simply in turning from sin to grace. To be complete, it should take place both outwardly and inwardly.[5]

A PERMANENT AND NATURAL SPIRITUAL CONDITION

When the soul is once turned toward God,[6] it finds a wonderful easiness in continuing steadfast in conversion. The longer it remains converted—[that is,

59

turned toward God], the nearer it gets to God and the more firmly it clings to Him. The nearer it gets to Him, the more it is removed, as an inevitable consequence, from the things of itself [and the flesh] that are contrary to Him. This results in it being so deeply established in conversion that this [spiritual] condition becomes permanent and natural.[7]

Now, we must not suppose that this [condition] is brought about by the soul's violent exertion of its own powers, for it does not have the ability to do so. Even with the help of divine grace, your soul should not attempt to do anything other than withdraw itself from external objects and turn inward. After that, it has nothing further to do than to continue holding firmly to God.[8]

GOD HAS AN ATTRACTIVE VIRTUE

God has an *attractive virtue*[9] that draws the soul more and more powerfully to Him. As He does, He purifies [the soul]. It is the same way as when the sun draws unclean water upward. As the water gradually ascends, its basic nature is elevated and made pure [as the unclean things in it fall away]. Now the only way the water contributes to its ascent is by being passive, but the soul cooperates freely and voluntarily.[10]

This method of turning the thoughts and feelings inward is very easy and advances the soul naturally and without effort, because God is our center.[11] Therefore, our center[12] always exerts a very powerful attraction.[13] And the more spiritual and exalted [we perceive it to be],[14] the more forceful and irresistible are its attractions.

THE LAW OF CENTRAL TENDENCY

In addition to the attracting virtue of the center, there is in each of us a strong tendency to reunite with our center—[that is, with God]. The strength and activity of this tendency is in proportion to the spirituality and perfection of the person.[15]

As soon as anything is turned toward its center, it moves toward it extremely fast,[16] unless some invincible object holds it back. A stone held in the hand is no sooner let loose[17] than by its own weight it falls toward its center—[that is, the center of the earth].[18] In the same way, when water and fire[19] are unobstructed they flow without interruption toward their center.[20] Now, when the soul's efforts to withdraw itself inward brings it into the influence of this [law of] *central tendency*, it falls gradually without any other force than the weight of love into its proper center—[God]. The more passive and tranquil the soul remains, and the freer it is from self-effort, the more rapidly it advances, because the drawing power of God is unobstructed and has full freedom of action. [21] [[22]]

DEVELOP A GREAT ABILITY TO WITHDRAW INWARD

All our attention should, therefore, be directed toward developing the greatest amount of ability to withdraw inward. We should not be discouraged by the difficulties we encounter in this exercise, which God will soon reward with an abundant supply of grace that will make it perfectly easy. Provided, of course, we are faithful in meekly *withdrawing* our hearts from outward distractions and occupations, and returning to our center with *affections* full of tenderness and peacefulness.[23] If at any time our passions are raging, a gentle retreat

61

inward to an [always] present God will easily deaden them. Trying to overcome our passions in any other way arouses rather than subdues them.

[1] Original title: *On Perfect Conversion*

[2] Original words: *the creature*

[3] Acts 14:15, 26:8, 26:20

[4] Original words: *It is not perfect (however good and essential to salvation)*

[5] Original words: *from without inwardly*

[6] The law of the LORD is perfect, converting the soul: the testimony of the LORD is sure, making wise the simple. (Psalm 19:7)

[7] Original paragraph-sentence: *When once the soul is once turned toward God, it finds a wonderful facility in continuing steadfast in conversion; and the longer it remains thus converted, the nearer it approaches and the more firmly it adheres to God; and the nearer it draws to Him, it is of necessity the farther removed from the creature, which is so contrary to Him; so that it is so effectually established in conversion, that the state becomes habitual, and as it were natural.*

[8] Original paragraph-sentence: *Now, we must not suppose that this is effected by a violent exertion of its own powers; for it is not capable of, nor should it attempt any other co-operation with divine grace, than that of endeavoring to withdraw itself from external objects, and to turn inwards; after which it has nothing farther to do, than to continue firm in its adherence to God.*

[9] Goodness, righteousness, holiness

[10] Original paragraph-sentence: *God has an attractive virtue which draws the soul more and more powerfully to Himself, and in attracting, He purifies; just as it is with a gross vapor exhaled by the sun, which, as it gradually ascends, is rarified and rendered pure; the*

vapor, indeed, contributes to its ascent only by its passivity; but the soul co-operates freely and voluntarily.

[11] Original sentence: *This kind of introversion is very easy and advances the soul naturally, and without effort, because God is our centre.*

[12] The spirit of a man is the lamp of the LORD, Searching all the inner depths of his heart. (Proverbs 20:27)

[13] Original words: *attractive virtue*

[14] Original words: *it is*

[15] Original sentence: *But besides the attracting virtue of the centre, there is, in every creature, a strong tendency to reunion with its centre, which is vigorous and active in proportion to the spirituality and perfection of the subject.*

[16] Original words: *is precipitated towards it with extreme rapidity*

[17] Original word: *disengaged*

[18] Original words: *to the earth as to its center*

[19] Here Madame Guyon is probably thinking of wood burning in a fireplace—a common way of heating in her day—rather than a forest or grass fire.

[20] Original sentence: *so also water and fire, when unobstructed, flow incessantly towards their centre.*

[21] Original sentence: *Now, when the soul by its efforts to recollect itself, is brought into the influence of the central tendency, it falls gradually, without any other force than the weight of love, into its proper centre; and the more passive and tranquil it remains, and the freer from self-motion, the more rapidly it advances,*

because the energy of the central attractive virtue is unobstructed, and has full liberty for action.

[22] Comments of a previous editor—possibly from the 1800s: *This beautiful image comprehends the whole essence of the divine life, as understood by the teachers of the interior, and seems to contain as much truth as beauty. God is the great magnet of the soul, but of that only; and impurity or a mixture prevents His full attractive power. If there were nothing of the kind in the soul, it would rush, under this all-powerful attraction, with irresistible and instantaneous speed, to be lost in God. But many load themselves with goods, or seize some part of earth or self with so tenacious a grasp, that they spend their whole lives without advancing at more than a snail's pace towards their center; and it is only when God in love strikes their burden violently from their hands, that they begin to be conscious of the hindrance that detained them. If we will only suffer every weight to drop, and withdraw our hands from self, and every creature, there will be but little interval between our sacrifice and our resurrection. Some pious persons have objected to the passivity here expounded upon, as though the soul were required to become dead, like an inanimate object, in order that God might do His pleasure with it. But this objection will vanish if it be considered that the life of the soul is in the will, and that this condition of utter passivity implies the highest state of activity of the will, in willing without any cessation, and with all its powers, that the will of God shall be done in it, and by it, and through it. See this further insisted upon in chapter 21.*

[23] Original sentence: *All our care should therefore be directed towards acquiring the greatest degree of inward recollection; nor should we be discouraged by*

the difficulties we encounter in this exercise, which will soon be recompensed on the part of God, by such abundant supplies of grace, as will render it perfectly easy, provided we are faithful in meekly withdrawing our hearts from outward distractions and occupations, and returning to our centre, with affections full of tenderness and serenity.

12

PRAYING SILENTLY TO GOD[1]

Another and more exalted degree of prayer, the prayer of the simple presence of God, or of active meditation, of which very little is said, the subject being reserved for another treatise. How selfish activity merges here in an activity lively, full, abundant, divine, easy, and as it were natural. This state is far different from that idleness and passivity objected to by the opponents of the inner life. The subject illustrated by several comparisons. Transition to infused prayer, in which the fundamental, vital, activity of the soul is not lost, but is more abundantly and powerfully influenced (as are the faculties) by God. The ease of these methods of coming to God, and an exhortation to self abandonment.

Those who are faithful in the exercise of love and faithfulness to God as described in the previous chapter, are astonished to feel Him gradually taking possession of their whole being. They now enjoy a continual sense of His presence that has become natural to them.[2] This sense of His presence, as well as prayer, becomes the normal pattern of their life, almost like an unconscious habit. They soon feel an unusual peacefulness gradually spreading over all their thoughts and emotions. All their praying is now done in silence, during which God communicates a love that fills every part of them—a love that is the beginning of indescribable [3] blessedness.[4]

O that I were permitted to pursue this subject, and describe some stages of the endless series of [spiritual] conditions that result [through this method of prayer]! But I am writing this only for beginners and will, therefore, go no further. I will wait our Lord's time for developing [further] what may be appropriate to every stage.

STOP SELF-ACTION AND SELF-EXERTION

I must, however, urge you as a matter of the highest importance to cease from self-action and self-exertion, so that God Himself may act alone. He says by the mouth of His prophet David, "Be still and know that I am God."[5] But we are so infatuated with love and attachment for our own efforts, that we do not believe that something works at all unless we can feel, know, and see all its operations. We are ignorant of the fact that our inability to observe small details of God's work within us is caused by the swiftness of its progress, and that as the workings of God abound[6] more and more they absorb our works. This is the same as the way that the stars shine brightly before the sun rises, but gradually vanish as its light advances—becoming invisible not from a lack of light in themselves, but from the excess of light in the sun.[7]

The case is similar here. The strong and universal light [of God] absorbs all the little distinct lights of the soul, and they grow faint and disappear under the powerful influence of God's light, and self-activity is no longer distinguishable.

Those who accuse this prayer of being inactive make a great mistake—it's an accusation that can only come from inexperience. O! if they would but make some efforts toward experiencing [this method of prayer], they would soon become full of light and knowledge in relation to it.[8]

This appearance of inaction is, indeed, not the result of [spiritual] barrenness [or lack], but of abundance. This will be clearly perceived by the experienced soul, who will recognize that the silence is full and rich[9] because of plenty.

TWO KINDS OF PEOPLE WHO ARE SILENT IN PRAYER

There are two kinds of people who are silent in prayer.[10] One because they have nothing to say, the other because they have too much to say. The latter is the case in this state—silence is produced by excess [of an overflowing heart], and not by lack.

To die by drowning and to die of thirst are two widely different deaths—yet water may be said to be the cause of both. Abundance destroys in one case, and lack [destroys] in the other. In the same way, the fullness of grace stills the activity of self. Therefore, it is of the utmost importance to remain as silent as possible.

SILENT PRAYER LIKE AN INFANT FEEDING

The infant feeding at its mother's breast, is a lively illustration of our subject. The child begins to draw the milk by moving its little lips, but when its nourishment flows abundantly it is content to swallow without effort.

If it continues its self-activity, however, it will only choke itself, spill the milk, and be obliged to quit the breast.[11]

We must act in a similar manner. In the beginning of prayer by moving the lips with words of love.[12] But as soon as the milk of divine grace flows freely, we have nothing to do but in silence lovingly[13] drink of it. Then when it ceases to flow, again stir up your affections in the same way[14] the infant moves its lips. Whoever acts otherwise, cannot make the best use of this grace, which is given to draw the soul into *the rest of love*, and not to force it into a great amount[15] of self-effort.

Now what happens to the baby who gently and without effort drinks in the milk? Who would believe that it could so easily receive nourishment? Yet the more peacefully it feeds, the better it thrives. So what happens to this infant? It falls asleep on its mother's bosom. In the same way, the soul that is quiet and peaceful in prayer often sinks into a [sort of] mystical [or spiritual] slumber in which all of its powers are at rest. These experiences will continue until the soul is wholly adapted to this mystical slumber and begins to enjoy and anticipate this temporary state. So you see, in this gradual process the soul is led naturally without trouble, effort, skill, or study.[16]

GAIN THE KINGDOM WITHIN YOU BY LOVE

Your interior is not a stronghold to be taken by storm and violence, but a kingdom of peace that is gained only by love. So if you will pursue [by love] the little path I have pointed out, it will lead you to *infused prayer* [that is, to a condition in which prayer is implanted so deeply within you that it becomes a natural part of your life]. God demands nothing extraordinary nor too difficult. On the contrary, He is greatly pleased by a simple and childlike conduct.

SUBLIME ATTAINMENTS ARE THE EASIEST TO REACH

The most sublime[17] attainments in religion are the easiest to reach. The most necessary [Christian] requirements are the least difficult. It is the same in natural things. If you want to reach the sea, set sail[18] on a river and you will be taken[19] to it gradually[20] and without effort. If you want to go to God, follow this sweet and simple path and you will arrive at Him with an ease and swiftness that will amaze you.[21]

O IF YOU WOULD ONLY ONCE TRY THIS METHOD![22]

You would soon find that I have said far too little, and that your own experience will carry you infinitely beyond what I have told you! What is it you fear? Why do you not instantly cast yourself into the arms of Love, who only extended His arms on the Cross so that He might embrace you? What risk do you run in depending solely on God, and abandoning yourself wholly to Him? Ah! He will not deceive you, but He may bestow upon you an abundance beyond your highest hopes. Now those who expect to receive everything by their self-efforts,[23] may hear this rebuke of God by His prophet Isaiah, "Ye have wearied yourselves in the multiplicity of your ways, and have not said, let us rest in peace."[24]

[1] Original title: *Prayer of the Presence of God*

[2] For additional study on this subject, see *The Practice of the Presence of God* by Brother Lawrence, a *Pure Gold Classic* published by Bridge-Logos Publishers.

[3] *blessedness*: a state or quality of happiness, pleasure, or contentment.

[4] Original sentence: *The soul that is faithful in the exercise of love and adherence to God, as above described, is astonished to feel Him gradually taking possession of its whole being; it now enjoys a continual sense of that presence which is become as it were natural to it; and this, as well as prayer, becomes a matter of habit. It feels an unusual serenity gradually diffusing itself over all its faculties. Silence now constitutes its whole prayer; whilst God communicates an infused love, which is the beginning of ineffable blessedness.*

[5] Psalm 46:10

[6] *abound*: to be great in number or amount.

[7] Original paragraph: *We must, however, urge it as a matter of the highest import, to cease from self-action and self-exertion, that God Himself may act alone: He says by the mouth of His prophet David, "Be still and know that I am God." (*Psalm *xlvi. 10.) But the creature is so infatuated with love and attachment to its own working, that it does not believe that it works at all unless it can feel, know, and distinguish all its operations. It is ignorant that its inability minutely to observe the manner of its motion, is occasioned by the swiftness of its progress; and that the operations of God, abounding more and more, absorb those of the creature; just as we see that the stars shine brightly before the sun rises, but gradually vanish as His light*

advances, and become invisible, not from want of light in themselves, but from the excess of it in Him.

[8] Original paragraph: *Those greatly err, who accuse this prayer of inactivity, a charge that can only arise from inexperience. O! if they would but make some efforts towards the attainment of it, they would soon become full of light and knowledge in relation to it.*

[9] Original word: *unctuous*

[10] Original words: *keep silence*

[11] Original sentence: *but when its nourishment flows abundantly, it is content to swallow without effort; by any other course it would only hurt itself, spill the milk, and be obliged to quit the breast.*

[12] Original words: *of the affections*

[13] Original word: *sweetly*

[14] Original word: *as*

[15] Original words: *the multiplicity*

[16] Original paragraph: *But what becomes of the babe that thus gently and without exertion, drinks in the milk? Who would believe that it could thus receive nourishment? Yet the more peacefully it feeds, the better it thrives. What, I say, becomes of this infant? It drops asleep on its mother's bosom. So the soul that is tranquil and peaceful in prayer, sinks frequently into a mystic slumber, wherein all its powers are at rest, till it is wholly fitted for that state, of which it enjoys these transient anticipations. You see that in this process the soul is led naturally, without trouble, effort, art or study.*

[17] *sublime*: Of high spiritual, moral, or intellectual worth; not to be excelled, supreme.

[18] Original word: *embark*

[19] Original word: *conveyed*

[20] Original word: *insensibly*

[21] Original sentence: *Would you go to God, follow this sweet and simple path, and you will arrive at the desired object, with an ease and expedition that will amaze you.*

[22] Original sentence: *O that you would but once make the trial!*

[23] Original words: *all from themselves*

[24] Isaiah 57:10 (Vulgate Bible) — The Vulgate Bible is a Latin translation of the Bible made by the scholar Jerome, a saint of the Roman Catholic Church, in the fourth century. This translation was the standard Bible of the Western world until the Reformation. *Vulgate* comes from a Latin word meaning "common." Jerome's translation used the Latin of everyday speech.

13

RESTING BEFORE GOD[1]

On the rest before God present in the soul in a wonderful way. Fruits of this peaceful presence. Practical advice.

Having advanced this far, your soul needs no other preparation than its quietness. For now the great result of the constant presence of God, or rather the constant prayer [that brings forth His presence], begins to *saturate your soul almost without interruption.*[2] Your soul now enjoys transcendent blessedness,[3] and finds that God is more intimately present to it than it is to itself.

THE ONLY WAY TO FIND GOD

The only way to find God is to direct your thoughts and feelings inward.[4] No sooner do your eyes[5] close than your soul is absorbed[6] in prayer. You will be amazed at so great a blessing, and enjoy an internal conversation [with God] that external matters cannot interrupt.

The same may be said of this kind of prayer that is said of wisdom: "all good things come together with her."[7] For virtues[8] will flow from your soul into practice with so much sweetness and ease that they will appear natural to it, and the living spring [of the Holy Spirit][9] will break forth abundantly into a facility[10] for all goodness, and an insensibility to all evil.

DO NOT SEEK ANY OTHER METHOD OF PRAYER

Let your soul, therefore, remain faithful in this state. Beware of choosing or seeking any other method[11] whatever than this simple rest as preparation for any spiritual activity or prayer.[12] For the only business of your soul is to allow itself to be filled with this divine outpouring.[13] I want you to understand that I am not speaking of the preparations necessary for ordinances,[14] but of the most perfect interior state in which they can be received.[15]

¹ Original title: *On Rest Before God*

² Original sentence: *for now the presence of God, during the day, which is the great effect, or rather continuation of prayer, begins to be infused, and almost without intermission.*

³ Supreme happiness, pleasure, or contentment surpassing all others

⁴ Original words: *by introversion*

⁵ Original words: *the bodily eyes*

⁶ Original word: *wrapt*

⁷ Chapter 7, verse 11 from the Book of Wisdom, which is part of the Apocrypha. The Apocrypha consists of the 14 books of the Septuagint included in the Vulgate but considered uncanonical by Protestants because they are not part of the Hebrew Scriptures. The Roman Catholic canon accepts 11 of these books and includes them in the Douay Bible. The complete verse reads, "Now all good things came to me together with her, and innumerable riches through her hands."

⁸ Moral excellence, righteousness, and goodness

⁹ John 4:14, 7:38-39

¹⁰ *facility*: the ability to perform without apparent effort: ease, readiness, easiness, effortlessness.

¹¹ Original word: *disposition*

¹² Original words: *a preparative either to confession or communion, to action or prayer*

¹³ Original word: *effusion*

¹⁴ *ordinance*: a Christian rite, especially the Eucharist.

¹⁵ Original sentence: *I would not be understood to speak of the preparations necessary for ordinances, but of the most perfect interior disposition in which they can be received.*

14

THE NECESSITY OF
INNER SILENCE[1]

On inward silence; its reason; God recommends it. External silence, retirement and turning inward contribute to it.

> The Lord is in His holy temple; let all
> the earth keep silence before Him.[2]

The reason why inward silence is so necessary is that the Word, [Jesus Christ], is essential and eternal. Therefore, it requires that the attitude of our soul to some degree correspond to His nature in order to receive Him.[3] Now hearing is the sense by which we receive sounds, and it is passive rather than active—[that is], it admits sensation but doesn't transmit it. So if we would hear something, we must give attention to it with our ear, [the organ given to us to receive sound].[4] Christ, the eternal Word, who must be communicated to our soul to give it new life, requires the most intense attention to His voice whenever He wants to speak within us.

That is why the Scriptures so often urge us to listen and be attentive to the voice of God. Here are a few of the numerous exhortations that speak about this.[5]

Hearken unto Me, My people; and give ear unto Me, O My nation.[6]

Hear Me, all ye whom I carry in My bosom, and bear within My bowels.[7]

Hearken, O daughter! and consider, and incline thine ear; forget also thine own people, and thy father's house; So shall the king greatly desire thy beauty.[8]

FORGET SELF AND BE ATTENTIVE TO GOD

We must *forget ourselves* and all our *self-interest*, and listen and be attentive *to God*. These two simple actions, which are really passive attitudes, produce the love of the beauty that He Himself communicates—[indeed, that He Himself is].[9]

External silence is essential for cultivating and improving internal silence. Indeed, it is impossible for us to become truly internal—[that is, learn to seek Christ within], without loving silence and seclusion. God says by the mouth of His prophet, "I will lead her into solitude, and there will I speak to her heart."[10] Without question, being internally occupied with God is wholly incompatible with being externally busied with a thousand trifles.[11]

THE CURE FOR DISTRACTIONS

Whenever we lose our inward concentration because of a lack of physical or mental self-discipline,[12] we must immediately turn inward again. And we must repeat this process as often as our distractions return.[13] It is of little value[14] to be devout and withdrawn inwardly[15] for an hour or half hour, if [as a result] the unction[16] and spirit of prayer do not continue with us during the whole day.

[1] Original title: *On Interiour Silence*

[2] Habakkuk 2:20

[3] Original sentence: *The reason why inward silence is so indispensable, is, because the Word is essential and eternal, and necessarily requires dispositions in the soul in some degree correspondent to His nature, as a capacity for the reception of Himself.*

[4] Original sentence: *Hearing is a sense formed to receive sounds, and is rather passive than active, admitting, but not communicating sensation; and if we would hear, we must lend the ear for that purpose.*

[5] Original sentence: *Hence it is so frequently enjoined upon us in sacred writ, to listen and be attentive to the voice of God; I quote a few of the numerous exhortations to this effect:*

[6] Isaiah 51:4

[7] Isaiah 46:3 — Quotation is probably from the Douay Bible, which is an English translation of the Latin Vulgate Bible by Roman Catholic scholars. In the King James Version of the Bible, Isaiah 46:3 reads: *Hearken unto Me, O house of Jacob, and all the remnant of the house of Israel, which are borne by Me from the belly, which are carried from the womb.*

[8] Psalm 45:10-11a

[9] Original sentence: *We must forget ourselves, and all self-interest, and listen and be attentive* to God; *these two simple actions, or rather passive dispositions, produce the love of that beauty, which He Himself communicates.*

[10] Hosea 2:14, Vulgate or Douay Bible. KJV reads: *Therefore, behold, I will allure her, and bring her into the wilderness, and speak comfortably unto her.*

[11] Original sentence: *Outward silence is very requisite for the cultivation and improvement of inward; and, indeed, it is impossible we should become truly interior, without loving silence and retirement. God saith by the mouth of his prophet, "I will lead her into solitude, and there will I speak to her heart* (Hos. ii. 14, vulg.); *and unquestionably the being internally engaged with God is wholly incompatible with being externally busied about a thousand trifles.*

[12] Original words: *When, through weakness, we become as it were uncentered,*

[13] Original word: *recur*

[14] Original words: *It is a small matter*

[15] Original word: *recollected*

[16] anointing

15

GOD HIMSELF EXAMINES US

On the examination of conscience; how it is performed in this state, and that by God Himself. On the confession, contrition, and forgetfulness or remembrance of faults in this state. This is not applicable to the previous degree. Communion.

Self-examination should always precede confession,[1] but the way of doing it should be in keeping with the state of your soul.[2] Those who have advanced to the degree we have been describing,[3] should lay their whole souls open before God. He will not fail to enlighten them, and will enable them to see the specific[4] nature of their faults. This examination should be peaceful and quiet, and we should depend on God to find and reveal our sins to us, rather than by our own efforts and scrutiny.[5]

SELF-LOVE CALLS EVIL GOOD AND GOOD EVIL

When we examine ourselves by our own effort, self-love betrays us and causes us to make mistakes:[6]

we "call evil good, and good evil."[7] But when we expose our soul fully[8] before the Sun of Righteousness, His divine beams make even the smallest sins[9] visible. We must, therefore, forsake self-effort, and abandon our souls to God as much in examination as in confession.

When your soul has advanced to this degree[10] of prayer, no sin escapes the rebuke[11] of God. No sooner is it committed than it is rebuked by an inward burning and tender confusion—[a strong inward awareness that you have done wrong]. God's scrutiny is such that He allows[12] no evil to be concealed, and the only way [for you] is to turn simply to God, and bear His chastening and scourging.[13]

When God becomes the constant[14] examiner of your soul, it will no longer be able to examine itself.[15] If you remain faithful to the abandonment [of your soul to God],[16] experience will prove that it is much more effectively[17] explored by His divine light than by all your careful examination.[18]

BE AWARE OF THIS MISTAKE

If you follow these paths, you should be aware that there is now something concerning your confession in which you may make a mistake. When you begin to give an account of your sins [to God], instead of the regret and remorse you had been accustomed to feeling, you find that love and tranquility sweetly pervade and take possession of your soul. Now if you are not properly instructed, you may want to resist this sensation and try to develop a feeling of repentance because you have heard, and rightly so, that this is required. But be aware that if you do that, you will lose the genuine repentance, which is the *infused love* [that you feel], and which infinitely surpasses any effect produced by self-exertion. That love contains within itself all the feelings of regret, remorse, and repentance in a much higher perfection than if they were [separately and] distinctly felt.[19]

Do not attempt to do otherwise,[20] when God acts so excellently in and for you. To hate sin in this manner is to hate it as God does. The purest love is that which results from His immediate operation in our souls, so why should we then be so eager for self-exertion? Let us remain in the state He assigns us, in keeping with the instructions of the wise man: "Put your confidence in God; remain in quiet where He hath placed you."[21]

DIFFICULTY IN REMEMBERING YOUR FAULTS

Your soul, [that is, you], will also be amazed to find it difficult to remember any of your faults. This, however, should cause no uneasiness. First, because this inability to remember your faults is a proof of your having been cleansed from them. Also, in this degree of advancement it is best to forget whatever concerns you so that you may remember only God. Second, because when you need to confess your sins, God will not fail to make known to you your greatest faults, for then He Himself examines you. Your soul, therefore, will feel that the examination was more perfectly accomplished than it could possibly have been by all your own efforts.[22]

THESE INSTRUCTIONS NOT FOR THE PREVIOUS DEGREE OF PRAYER

These instructions, however, are completely unsuitable to the degrees [of prayer] preceding [this one]—those in which the soul continues in its active state. In those degrees it is right and necessary that in all things the soul should make a strong effort to examine itself and deal with its sins, in proportion to how far it has advanced. If you, however, have arrived at this more advanced state, I exhort you to follow these instructions, and not to vary your simple actions, even if you are going to receive communion[23] . Remain silent and allow God to act freely. He cannot be better received than by Himself.[24]

[1] Here Madame Guyon is speaking of confessing sins to a priest, as practiced in the Roman Catholic church, but self-examination before confession holds equally true when we are confessing our sins to God as in 1 John 1:5.

[2] Original words: *but the manner of it should be conformable to the state of the soul.*

[3] Original words: *The business of those that are advanced to the degree of which we now treat,*

[4] Original word: *peculiar*

[5] Original words: *and we should depend on God for the discovery and knowledge of our sins, rather than on the diligence of our own scrutiny.*

[6] Original words: *When we examine with effort, we are easily deceived, and betrayed by self-love into error:*

[7] Isaiah 5:20

[8] Original words: *we lie in full exposure*

[9] Original words: *render the smallest atoms*

[10] Original words: *When souls have attained to this species*

[11] Original word: *reprehension*

[12] Original words: *Such is the scrutiny of Him who suffers*

[13] Original words: *pain and correction He inflicts —* Hebrews 12:5-11

[14] Original word: *incessant*

[15] 1 Corinthian 4:3-4

[16] Original words: *and if it be faithful in its abandonment,*

[17] Original word: *effectually*

[18] Original words: *its own carefulness*

[19] Original paragraph: *Those who tread these paths should be informed of a matter respecting their confession, in which they are apt to err. When they begin to give an account of their sins, instead of the regret and contrition they had been accustomed to feel, they find that love and tranquility sweetly pervade and take possession of their souls: now those who are not properly instructed are desirous of resisting this sensation, and forming an act of contrition, because they have heard, and with truth, that this is requisite. But they are not aware that they thereby lose the genuine contrition, which is this infused love, and which infinitely surpasses any effect produced by self-exertion, comprehending the other acts in itself as in one principal act, in much higher perfection than if they were distinctly perceived.*

[20] Original words: *Let them not be troubled*

[21] Original text references Ecclesiastes 11:22, but no matching verse could be in any version of the Bible, including the Apocrypha.

[22] Original paragraph: *The soul will also be amazed at finding a difficulty in calling its faults to remembrance. This, however, should cause no uneasiness, first, because this forgetfulness of our faults is some proof of our purification from them, and, in this degree of advancement, it is best to forget whatever concerns ourselves that we may remember only God. Secondly, because, when confession is our duty, God will not fail to make known to us our greatest faults; for then He himself examines; and the soul will feel the end of examination more perfectly accomplished, than it could possibly have been by all our own endeavors.*

[23] The Lord's supper, covenant meal, etc.

[24] Original paragraph: *These instructions, however, would be altogether unsuitable to the preceding degrees, while the soul continues in its active state, wherein it is right and necessary that it should in all things exert itself, in proportion to its advancement. As to those who have arrived at this more advanced state, I exhort them to follow these instructions, and not to vary their simple occupations even on approaching the communion; let them remain in silence, and suffer God to act freely. He cannot be better received than by Himself.*

16

USE OF READING AND VOCAL PRAYERS[1]

On reading and vocal prayers; they should be limited. Not to be used against our internal drawing, unless they are obligated.

The way to read [the Scriptures or spiritual books] in this advanced state is to stop reading the moment you feel yourself drawn inward. Always remain quiet and read only a little at a time—and always stop reading when you feel an attraction to turn inward.[2]

GIVING YOURSELF TO THE HOLY SPIRIT'S LEADING

Now that your soul has been called to a state of inward silence, you should not burden yourself with vocal prayers. If you do pray vocally, and find it difficult to do and are attracted to inward silence, do not resist by continuing to pray outwardly. Yield to the inward drawing—unless, of course, you are under some obligation to say vocal prayers.[3] In any other case, it is better not to be burdened with and tied to repetition of set forms [of prayer], but to give yourself up completely to the leading of the Holy Spirit.[4] In this way, every kind of devotion is fulfilled to the highest degree.[5]

[1] Original title: On Reading and Vocal Prayers

[2] Original paragraph: *The method of reading in this state, is to cease when you feel yourself recollected, and remain in stillness, reading but little, and always desisting when thus internally attracted.*

[3] Madame Guyon is undoubtedly referring to practices in the Roman Catholic church that required a person to pray certain prayers outwardly, sometimes as penance for sins after confessing them to a priest.

[4] Romans 8:26

[5] Original paragraph: *The soul that is called to a state of inward silence, should not encumber itself with vocal prayers; whenever it makes use of them, and finds a difficulty therein, and an attraction to silence, let it not use constraint by persevering, but yield to the internal drawings, unless the repeating such prayers be a matter of obligation. In any other case, it is much better not to be burdened with and tied down to the repetition of set forms, but wholly given up to the leadings of the Holy Spirit; and in this way every species of devotion is fulfilled in a most eminent degree.*

17

THE SPIRIT NOW MAKES YOUR PETITIONS[1]

On petitions: those which are self-originated cease, and their place is supplied by those of the Spirit of God. Abandonment and faith necessary here.

[In this advanced state], you should not be surprised at being unable to offer up to God petitions that you formerly made with ease.[2] For now the Spirit that helps you in your weaknesses makes intercession for you according to the will of God:[3] "for we know not what we should pray for as we ought; but the Spirit itself maketh intercession for us with groanings which cannot be uttered."[4] You must, therefore, agree with[5] the plans of God, which are intended to remove from you all of your own activities so that His may replace them.[6]

book

BE ATTACHED TO NOTHING THAT TURNS YOU FROM GOD

So let this be done in you. And do not allow yourself to be attached to anything that in any measure turns you aside from what God desires of you, no matter how good it may appear, for it is no longer good to you. His divine will is preferable to every other good. Therefore, shake off all self-interest, and live by faith and abandonment. This is when *genuine* faith begins to truly operate.[7]

[1] Original title: *The Spirit Indites Our Petitions*

[2] Original words: *The soul should not be surprised at feeling itself unable to offer up to God such petitions as had formerly been made with facility;*

[3] Original words: *for now the Spirit maketh intercession for it according to the will of God; that Spirit which helpeth our infirmities*

[4] Romans 8:26

[5] Original word: *second,* which was undoubtedly used in the sense of *endorse* or *agree with.*

[6] Original sentence: *We must second the designs of God, which tend to divest us of all our own operations, that His may be substituted in their place.*

[7] Original paragraph: *Let this, then, be done in you; and suffer not yourself to be attached to anything, however good it may appear; it is no longer such to you, if it in any measure turns you aside from what God desires of you. For the divine will is preferable to every other good. Shake off, then, all self-interest, and live by faith and abandonment; here it is that genuine faith begins truly to operate.*

18

What to Do When a Fault Is Committed[1]

On faults committed in the state. We must turn from them to God without trouble or discouragement. The contrary course weakens us and is opposed to the practice of humble souls.

If you should be distracted [from prayer] by external matters or commit a fault, you must instantly turn inward. Since these matters or fault caused you to depart from the inward presence of God, you should turn back toward Him as soon as possible. If He chastises you in any way [for your departure], accept it [willingly and learn from it].[2]

It is extremely important that you guard against being annoyed or irritated with yourself because of your faults. Such feelings spring from a secret root of pride and a love of your own excellence. You get [upset and] hurt by seeing what you [really] are.[3]

If you become discouraged, you will be weakened even more. And if you reflect on your imperfections, you'll be disappointed with yourself [and even humiliated],[4] which is often worse than the imperfections themselves.

DEFECTS AND FAILINGS TURN THE HUMBLE SOUL TO GOD

Truly humble souls are not surprised at their defects or failings. The more miserable they see themselves, the more they abandon themselves to God and press toward a more intimate relationship with Him,[5] because they have seen how much they need His aid. So we should be persuaded to act this way rather than any other, as God Himself has said,[6] "I will instruct thee and teach thee in the way which thou shalt go: I will guide thee with Mine eye."[7]

[1] Original title: *On Faults Committed*

[2] Original paragraph: *Should we either wander among externals, or commit a fault, we must instantly turn inwards; for having departed thereby from God, we should as soon as possible turn toward Him, and suffer the penalty which He inflicts.*

[3] Original paragraph: *It is of great importance to guard against vexation on account of our faults; it springs from a secret root of pride, and a love of our own excellence; we are hurt at feeling what we are.*

[4] Original words: *If we become discouraged, we are the more enfeebled; and from our reflections on our imperfections, a chagrin arises,*

[5] Philippians 3:14

[6] Original paragraph: *The truly humble soul is not surprised at its defects or failings; and the more miserable it beholds itself, the more it abandons itself to God, and presses for a more intimate alliance with Him, seeing the need it has of His aid. We should the rather be induced to act thus, as God Himself has said,*

[7] Psalm 32:8

19

OVERCOMING DISTRACTIONS AND TEMPTATIONS[1]

On distractions and temptations; the remedy for them is to turn to God. This is the practice of the [ancient] saints, and there is danger in any other way.

Struggling directly with distractions and temptations will strengthen rather than weaken them, and will draw your soul away from that devotional attention to God that should always be its sole occupation. We should simply turn away from the evil and draw even closer to God. When a little child [is sitting on its mother's lap and] imagines that she sees a monster [lurking in the shadows of the room], she does not wait to fight with it, and will hardly look at it, but will quickly draw closer to her mother in [full] assurance that she is safe [in her mother's arms].[2] "God is in the midst of her;" says the Psalmist, "she shall not be moved: God shall help her, and that right early" (Psalm 46:4).

ATTACKING YOUR ENEMIES WILL DEFEAT YOU

If we do otherwise, and in our weakness attempt to attack our enemies, we will frequently find ourselves wounded, if not totally defeated. But by remaining in the simple presence of God, we will find instant supplies of strength for our support. This was the resource of David: "I have set," says he, "the LORD always before me: because He is at my right hand, I shall not be moved. Therefore my heart is glad, and my glory rejoiceth: my flesh also shall rest in hope" (Psalm 16:8-9). And it is said in Exodus, "The LORD shall fight for you, and ye shall hold your peace" (Exodus 14:14).

[1] Original title: *On Distractions and Temptations*

[2] Original text: *A direct struggle with distractions and temptations rather serves to augment them, and withdraws the soul from that adherence to God, which should ever be its sole occupation. We should simply turn away from the evil, and draw yet nearer to God. A little child, on perceiving a monster, does not wait to fight with it, and will scarcely turn its eyes toward it, but quickly shrinks into the bosom of its mother, in assurance of its safety.*

20

Prayer Divinely Explained

Prayer divinely explained as a devotional sacrifice, signified by offering of incense. Annihilation [of self] in this sacrifice. Solidity and fruit of this prayer according to the Gospel.

Both devotion and sacrifice are included in prayer, which [the apostle] John says is [mingled with an] incense whose smoke ascends up before God.[1] Therefore it says in the Apocalypse, [the Book of Revelation], "And another angel came and stood at the altar, having a golden censer; and there was given unto him much incense, that he should offer it with the prayers of all saints upon the golden altar which was before the throne. And the smoke of the incense, which came with the prayers of the saints, ascended up before God out of the angel's hand" (Revelation 8:3-4).[2]

WHAT PRAYER IS

Prayer is the outpouring[3] of the heart in the presence of God: "I . . . have poured out my soul before the LORD," said the mother of Samuel.[4] The prayer of the wise men at the feet of Christ in the stable of Bethlehem was signified by the incense they offered.[5]

Prayer is a certain, [an indisputable], warmth of love that melts, dissolves, and elevates the soul and causes it to ascend unto God.[6] As the soul is melted, fragrances[7] rise from it. These sweet outpourings come[8] from the consuming fire of love within it.

This is illustrated in the Canticles[9] where the spouse says, "While the king sitteth at his table, my spikenard sendeth forth the smell thereof" (Song of Songs 1:12). The table is [symbolic of] the center of the soul, and when God is there and we know how to remain near and abide with Him, His sacred presence gradually dissolves the hardness of our soul. As our soul melts, fragrance pours forth. So when the Beloved saw the soul of his spouse melt when he spoke, he said of her,[10] "Who is this that cometh out of the wilderness like pillars of smoke, perfumed with myrrh and frankincense?" (Song of Songs 3:6).

WHEN SELF IS DONE AWAY WITH, THE SOUL ASCENDS TO GOD

By giving up *self* to the destroying and annihilating power of divine love, the soul ascends to God. This state of sacrifice in which the soul allows *self*[11] to be destroyed and annihilated so that it may submit itself[12] to the sovereignty of God is essential to [true] Christianity. As it is written, "the power of the Lord is great, and He is honoured of the lowly."[13] By the

110

destruction of *self*, we acknowledge the supreme existence of God. We must cease to exist in *self* in order that the Spirit of the Eternal Word may exist in us. It is by giving up our own life, that we give place to His coming. And [it is] in dying to ourselves, that He lives in us.

We must surrender our whole being to Christ Jesus, and cease to live any longer in ourselves so that He may become our life: "For ye are dead, and your life is hid with Christ in God" (Colossians 3:3). "Pass ye into Me," sayeth God, "all ye who earnestly seek after Me."[14] But how do[15] we pass into God? The only way is[16] by leaving and forsaking ourselves so that we may be lost in Him. This can be brought about[17] only by annihilation, which is the true prayer of adoration, and which renders unto God alone all "blessing, and honor, and glory, and power . . . forever and ever."[18]

THE PRAYER OF TRUTH

This prayer of truth is that which "worship[s] the Father in spirit and in truth."[19] *"In spirit"* because we enter into the purity of that Spirit who prays within us, and are drawn away from our own carnal and human methods. *"In truth,"* because we enter into[20] the truth of the all of God, and the nothing of us.[21]

There are but these two truths, the *all* and the *nothing*—everything else is false. We can pay due honor to the *all* of God, only in [our own *nothingness*], our own *annihilation*. The instant this is[22] accomplished, God, who never allows a void in nature, instantly fills us with Himself.

111

The blessings the soul receives from this method of prayer

Ah! if we only understood the virtues and the blessings that the soul receives from this [method of] prayer, we would not be willing to do anything else. It is the hidden treasure, the pearl of great price,[23] and those who find it quickly[24] sell all they have to buy it. It is the "well of living water springing up into everlasting life."[25] It is the worship of God "in spirit and in truth."[26] Further, it is the full performance of the purest precepts of the Christian gospel.[27]

The kingdom of God is within us

Jesus Christ tells us positively[28] that the "kingdom of God is within us."[29] This is true in two ways. First, when God becomes so fully Master and Lord in us that nothing resists His dominion, [His sovereignty], then our interior is His kingdom. Second, when we possess God who is the Supreme Good, we possess His kingdom also. In these two things there is fullness of joy, and by them we arrive at the purpose for which we were created.[30] Thus it is said, "to serve God is to reign."[31] Without a doubt, the purpose of our creation is to enjoy God—and to enjoy Him in this life. But, alas! who thinks of enjoying Him?[32]

[1] Original sentence: *Both devotion and sacrifice are comprehended in prayer, which, according to St. John is an incense, the smoke whereof ascendeth unto God;*

[2] Original Scripture quotation was only a partial paraphrase: *"unto the angel was given much incense, that he should offer it with the prayers of all saints."*

[3] Original word: *effusion*

[4] 1 Samuel 1:15

[5] Matthew 2:11

[6] Original sentence: *Prayer is a certain warmth of love, melting, dissolving, and sublimating the soul, and causing it to ascend unto God,*

[7] Original word: *odors*

[8] Original words: *exhalations proceed*

[9] Song of Songs

[10] Original sentence: *hence it is, that the beloved says of his spouse, in seeing her soul melt when he spoke,*

[11] Original word: *itself*

[12] Original words: *pay homage*

[13] From the Apocrypha, Ecclesiasticus 3:20

[14] From the Apocrypha, paraphrase of Ecclesiasticus 24:19—*"Come unto me all ye that be desirous of me."*

[15] Original words: *is it*

[16] Original words: *In no way but*

[17] Original word: *effected*

[18] Revelation 5:13b

[19] John 4:23

[20] Original words: *are thereby placed in*

[21] Original words: *the creature*

[22] Original words: *which is no sooner*

[23] Matthew 13:44-46

[24] Original word: *freely* — probably in sense of immediately without restrain

[25] John 4:10b, 14

[26] John 4:23-24

[27] Original words: *purest evangelical precepts* — the word *evangelical* means "of, or relating to, or in accordance with the Christian gospel."

[28] Original word: *assures*

[29] Luke 17:21

[30] Original words: *wherein there is fulness of joy, and where we attain the end of our creation.*

[31] Source of quotation unknown.

[32] Original words: *The end of our creation, indeed, is to enjoy God, even in this life; but, alas! who thinks of it?* In Madame Guyon's day, Christianity for the common people was a religion that was an oppressive and burdensome necessity. Anyone found actually enjoying Christianity and God, and especially loving and enjoying Jesus Christ, was immediately suspected of being spiritual, mentally, or emotionally abnormal in some way, and a threat to the teachings of the "true church." It was said that Madame Guyon was imprisoned by her church in the Paris Bastille because "she loved God too much."

21

THE SOUL IS ACTIVE WHEN
SELF IS STILL

The objections of laziness and inactivity made to this form of prayer fully met, and the truth shown that the soul acts nobly, forcibly, calmly, quickly, freely, simply, sweetly, temperately, and certainly; but in dependence upon God, and moved by His Holy Spirit: the restless and selfish activity of nature being destroyed, and the life of God communicated by union with Him.

When some people hear about the prayer of silence, they falsely imagine *that the soul remains dull, dead, and inactive.* But [just the opposite is true]. Without question the soul acts more nobly and more extensively than it has ever done before. God Himself is its mover, and He now energizes and directs its activities by His Spirit.[1] The apostle Paul speaks of it as being[2] "led by the Spirit of God."[3]

EZEKIEL'S VISION OF THE WHEELS

This does not mean[4] that we should cease from action, but that we should act through the internal instrument[5] of His grace—[the Holy Spirit]. This is splendidly illustrated[6] by the prophet Ezekiel's vision of the wheels, which had a living Spirit. Wherever[7] the Spirit wanted to go, they went. They ascended and descended as they were moved, for the Spirit of life was in them, and they did not return [to where they had been] when they went.[8] Like the wheels, the soul should be submissive[9] to the will of that animating Spirit who is in it, and painstakingly[10] faithful to follow only as He[11] moves. These movements never reflect backwards upon the person or *self*, but go forward in an unceasing advance toward the goal [of God's purpose for the soul].[12]

This *activity* of the soul takes place[13] with the utmost peace.[14] When the soul acts on its own, the act is forced and inhibited. Therefore it's easy to tell when the soul is acting upon its own—[it cannot pray easily and freely].[15] When the action is under the influence of the Spirit of grace, however, it is so free, so easy, and so natural, that it almost seems as if we did not act at all. "He brought me forth also into a large place; He delivered me, because He delighted in me."[16]

THE POWERFUL ACTION OF THE CENTRAL TENDENCY

The moment the soul is in its central tendency,[17] — or, in other words, has turned [toward your center] by withdrawing into itself—the attraction of that center becomes a most powerful activity, [or action, upon the soul], infinitely surpassing in energy every other kind [of activity]. Nothing, indeed, can equal the swiftness of this tendency [of the soul] to [move to] the center—[where the Holy Spirit dwells].[18] And although [this is] an activity, it is so noble, so peaceful, so full of tranquility, so natural, and so spontaneous, that it appears to the soul as if it were not an activity[19] at all.

When a wheel rolls slowly we can easily identify its parts. But when it moves rapidly,[20] we can distinguish nothing. In the same way, the soul that rests in God has an activity [that is] exceedingly noble and elevated, yet altogether peaceful. And the more peaceful it is, the swifter it moves,[21] because it is given up to that Spirit by whom it is moved and directed.

GOD HIMSELF IS THE ATTRACTING SPIRIT

This attracting Spirit is none other than God Himself. In drawing us, He causes us to run to Him. How well did the spouse understand this when she said, "Draw me, we will run after thee."[22]

Draw me unto Thee, O my divine center, by the secret springs of my existence, and all my powers and senses shall follow Thee!

This simple attraction is both an ointment to heal and a perfume to allure. "We follow," saith she, "the fragrance of thy perfumes."[23] Although this is such a *powerful* attraction, the soul follows it freely and without restraints, for it is as equally delightful as it is forceful.[24] While it attracts by its power, it carries us away by its sweetness. "Draw me," says the spouse, "and we will run after thee." She speaks of and to herself: "*draw me*,"—note the oneness of the center that is drawn [to the Holy Sprit]![25] "*We will run*,"—note

117

the communication and agreement of all the senses and powers in following the attraction of the center!

THIS METHOD OF PRAYER PROMOTES THE HIGHEST ACTIVITY

So instead of encouraging laziness, we promote the highest activity. We do this by repeatedly teaching[26] a *total dependence on the Spirit of God* as our source of activity.[27] For it is in Him and by Him alone that "we live, and move, and have our being."[28] This humble[29] dependence on the Spirit of God is essential,[30] and will soon cause the soul to regain the unity and simplicity in which it was [originally] created.[31]

We must forsake, therefore, our great variety of activities[32] in order to enter into the simplicity and unity of God, in whose image we were originally created.[33] "The Spirit is one and manifold,"[34] and God's unity does not preclude[35] His multiplicity. We enter into His unity when we are united to His Spirit, and by that means have one and the same spirit with Him.[36] We are able to fulfill all the various outward requirements of His will[37] without any departure from our state of union.

In this way, when we are wholly moved by the divine Spirit who is infinitely active, our activity is naturally[38] more energetic than when it[39] is merely our own. We must yield ourselves to the guidance of [the Holy Spirit's] wisdom, "for wisdom is more moving than any motion."[40] By remaining dependent[41] upon His[42] action, our activity will be truly efficient.

GOD BREATHED HIS NATURE INTO US

"All things were made by the Word, and without Him was not anything made, that was made."[43] God originally formed us in His own image and likeness—

He breathed into us the Spirit of His Word.[44] God's image was contained in that breath of life that He gave us at our creation—it was by that breath that He shared His nature with us.[45] Now, this LIFE is one, simple, pure, intimate, and always fruitful.

The devil, however, has broken and deformed the divine image in the soul by sin. Therefore, Christ,[46] the same Word whose Spirit was inbreathed at our creation,[47] is absolutely necessary for our soul's[48] renovation. It is necessary that it be Christ[49] because He is the express image of His Father. No image can be repaired by its own efforts, but must remain passive for that purpose under the hand of the workman.

BE ACTIVELY SENSITIVE

Our *activity* should, therefore, consist in *being always* sensitive[50] to divine impressions, and receptive[51] to all the operations of the eternal Word.[52] While a tablet is unsteady [and often moving], the painter is unable to produce a correct picture upon it. In the same way, every movement of *self* can produce incorrect lines and shapes.[53] Such movement interrupts the work and defeats the design of this adorable Painter. So we must remain in peace, and move only when He moves us. Jesus Christ has life in Himself,[54] and He must give life to every living thing.

The Spirit of God's Church[55] is the Spirit of the divine movement—[that is, the movement of the Holy Spirit]. Is the Church[56] idle, barren, or unfruitful? No— she acts, but her activity is dependent[57] upon the Spirit of God, who moves and governs her. It should be the same in[58] her members. To be[59] spiritual children of the [mystical] Church—[the true body of Christ], they must be led[60] by the Spirit.[61]

119

THE VALUE OF ACTIVITY DEPENDS ON THE SOURCE

Since all activity is valuable only in proportion to the quality and worth of the source or force motivating or generating it, this activity [by the Holy Spirit] is incontestably [higher and] more noble than any other.[62] Actions produced by the Holy Spirit are *divine*, but our actions, however good or virtuous they may seem to be, are only *human*—even when accompanied by grace.[63]

Jesus Christ said that He has life in Himself.[64] All other human beings have only a borrowed life, but the Word, [Jesus Christ], has life in Himself. Since that life imparts His nature, He desires to bestow it upon us.[65] We should, therefore, make room for that life to come in, and this can only be done by the ejection and loss of the Adamic life, [the old man],[66] and the suppression of *self*-activity. This agrees with the assertion of the apostle Paul, ""If any man be in Christ, he is a new creature: old things are passed away; behold, all things are become new."[67] This state, however, can be accomplished only by dying to ourselves and to all our [*self*]-activity, so that the [*divine*]-activity of God may take its place.

RATHER THAN PROHIBITING ACTIVITY, WE PRESCRIBE IT

Instead of prohibiting activity, therefore, we prescribe it—but only in absolute dependence on the Spirit of God, so that His activity may take the place of our own. This can only occur by our consent, and it is a simultaneous occurrence—as we lessen our own activity, the activity of God little by little replaces it [until all is His activity and there is none of ours].[68]

Jesus gave an example[69] this [as recorded] in the gospel [of Luke]. Martha did what was right, but because she did it in her own spirit Jesus rebuked her. Our spirit is [often] restless and disturbed, and for that reason we accomplish little even though we seem to do a great deal.[70] "Jesus . . . said unto her, Martha, Martha, thou art careful and troubled about many things: But one thing is needful: and Mary hath chosen that good part, which shall not be taken away from her."[71] What was it Mary had chosen? Rest, tranquility, and peace. She had apparently ceased to act so that the Spirit of Christ might act in her—she had ceased to live so that Christ might be her life.[72]

NECESSARY TO RENOUNCE OURSELVES

This shows how necessary it is to renounce ourselves and all our [*self-*]activity, to follow Christ, for we cannot follow Him if the source of our activity is not[73] His Spirit. Now that His Spirit may gain entrance, it is necessary that our own [spirit] should be surrendered to it.[74] "He that is joined unto the Lord," says the apostle Paul, "is one spirit."[75] And David said it was good for him to draw near unto the Lord, and to put his trust in him.[76] What is this drawing near? It is the beginning of [divine] union [between you and Christ].

SEVERAL STAGES OF DIVINE UNION

Divine union has [several stages]: its beginning, its progress, its achievement, and its completion. The beginning stage is an inclination toward God—when the soul is directed inward in the manner described before, it gets within the influence of the central attraction and develops an eager desire for union [with

121

God]. As it progresses nearer and nearer to Him it clings increasingly to Him. Finally, it achieves its goal and becomes one spirit with Him. It is then that the soul that had wandered from God completes its return to the end [or purpose] for which it was created.[77]

This is God's way of moving us from one stage to the next, and it is a way that we must necessarily [and voluntarily] enter if we desire union with the Spirit of Christ.[78] The apostle Paul says, "If any man have not the spirit of Christ, he is none of His."[79] To be Christ's, therefore, we must be filled with His Spirit, and emptied of our own [self-life]. In the same passage [of text], the Apostle proves the necessity of this divine influence. "As many," says he, "as are led by the Spirit of God, they are the sons of God."[80]

The Spirit of divine parentage,[81] then, is the Spirit of divine action—the one and same Spirit. Paul therefore adds, "Ye have not received the spirit of bondage again to fear; but ye have received the Spirit of adoption whereby ye cry Abba, Father."[82] This Spirit is none other than the Spirit of Christ, through which we participate in His [family] relationship[83] [to God]: "The Spirit itself beareth witness with our spirit, that we are the children of God."[84]

When the soul yields itself to the influence of this blessed Spirit, it receives[85] the witness[86] of it being a child of God.[87] And with superabundant joy, it feels also that it has not received the spirit of bondage but of liberty, even the liberty of the children of God. It then finds that it *acts freely and sweetly*, and yet with strength and certainty.

THE SPIRIT OF DIVINE ACTION

The Spirit of divine action is so necessary in all things, that in the same passage [of text] the apostle Paul states the necessity of it even when we pray, because we do not know what we should pray for.[88] "The Spirit," says he, "also helpeth our infirmities: for we know not what we should pray for as we ought; but the Spirit itself maketh intercession for us, with groanings which cannot be uttered."[89] This is plain enough. If we do not know what we need, nor how to pray as we should for those things that are necessary, and if the Spirit who is in us and to whom we surrender ourselves must ask for us, should we not permit Him to express His unutterable groanings in our behalf?

THE SPIRIT OF THE WORD

This Spirit is the Spirit of the Word, who is always heard, as He Himself says, "I knew that thou hearest me always."[90] If we freely admit this Spirit to pray and intercede for us, we also will always be heard. Why [is that so]? Let us learn from the same great apostle, that skillful mystic, and master of the interior life, where he adds, "He that searcheth the heart, knoweth what is the mind of the Spirit; because He maketh intercession for the saints according to the will of God"[91] That is to say, the Spirit demands only what is according[92] to the will of God. The will of God is that we should be saved and that we should become perfect: He, therefore, intercedes for all that is necessary for our perfection.

WHY BURDEN OURSELVES UNNECESSARILY?

Why, then, should we burden ourselves with unnecessary[93] cares, and weary ourselves with a multitude of activities,[94] without ever saying [to God],

"Let us rest in peace."[95] God Himself invites us to cast all our care upon Him.[96] In Isaiah, He complains with indescribable goodness that the soul had expended its powers and its treasures on a thousand external objects, when there was so little it had to do to obtain all it needed or desired. "Wherefore do ye spend money for that which is not bread? and your labour for that which satisfieth not? hearken diligently unto Me, and eat ye that which is good, and let your soul delight itself in fatness."[97]

Be silent before God

Oh! If we but knew the blessedness of listening attentively[98] to God, and how greatly the soul is strengthened by such a course! "Be silent, O all flesh, before the Lord"[99] Everything must cease as soon as He appears. But to encourage us to abandon ourselves still further without reservation,[100] God speaks through the same prophet and assures that we need fear nothing because He takes a very special care of us. "Can a woman forget her sucking child, that she should not have compassion on the son of her womb? Yea, they may forget, yet will not I forget thee."[101] O words full of comfort [and encouragement]![102] Who [of us] after that will fear to abandon ourselves[103] wholly to the guidance of God?

¹ Original words: *its mover, and it now acts by the agency of His Spirit.*

² Original words: *St. Paul would have us*

³ Romans 8:14

⁴ Original words: *It is not meant*

⁵ Original word: *agency*

⁶ Original words: *finely represented*

⁷ Original words: *and whithersoever*

⁸ Original words: *and they returned not when they went.* Ezekiel 1:18-21

⁹ Original word: *equally subservient*

¹⁰ Original words: *scrupulously*

¹¹ Original word: *that*

¹² Original sentence: *These motions never tend to return in reflections on the creatures or self; but go forward in an incessant approach toward the end.*

¹³ Original words: *is attended*

¹⁴ Original word: *tranquility*

¹⁵ Original sentence: *When it acts of itself, the act is forced and constrained, and, therefore, it is more easily distinguished;*

¹⁶ Psalm 18:19

¹⁷ The center toward which the soul tends to fall naturally. See chapter 11.

¹⁸ Original words: *When the soul is in its central tendency, or in other words, is returned through recollection into itself, from that moment, the central attraction becomes a most potent activity, infinitely surpassing in energy every other species. Nothing,*

indeed, can equal the swiftness of this tendency to the centre;

[19] Original words: *it were none*

[20] Original words: *its motion is rapid*

[21] Original words: *is its course*

[22] Song of Songs 1:4

[23] Probably a paraphrase using words from Song of Songs 1:3 and 1:4.

[24] Original words: *it is followed by the soul freely, and without constraint; for it is equally delightful as forcible*

[25] This is much like the Psalmist saying, "Bless the Lord, O my soul." - Psalm 103:1.

[26] Original word: *inculcating*

[27] Original words: *moving principle*

[28] Acts 17:28a

[29] Original word: *meek*

[30] Original words: *indispensably necessary*

[31] Original words: *and causes the soul shortly to attain the unity and simplicity in which it was created.*

[32] Original words: *multifarious activity*

[33] Original word: *formed* - Genesis 1:27

[34] Paraphrase of verse 7:22 from the Wisdom of Solomon in the Apocrypha—*"For wisdom which is the worker of all things, taught me; for in her is an understanding spirit, holy, one only, manifold . . ."*

[35] *preclude*: prevent, make impossible

[36] John 10:30, 17:21

[37] Original words: *and we are multiplied in respect to the outward execution of His will,*

[38] Original words: *must, indeed, be*

[39] Original words: *that which*

[40] Apocrypha, Wisdom of Solomon 7:24

[41] Original words: *abiding in dependence*

[42] Original word: *its*

[43] John 1:3

[44] Genesis 1:27, 2:7

[45] Original words: *that breath of Life which He gave us at our creation, in the participation whereof the image of God consisted.*

[46] Original words: *the agency of*

[47] Colossians 1:16-17

[48] Original word: *its*

[49] Original words: *It was necessary that it should be He,*

[50] Original word: *susceptibility*

[51] Original word: *pliability*

[52] Original words: *consist in* placing ourselves *in a state of susceptibility to divine impressions, and pliability to all the operations of the Eternal Word.*

[53] Original words: *is productive of erroneous lineaments*

[54] John 5:26

[55] Original words: *the Church of God*

[56] Original word: *she*

[57] Original words: *in dependence*

[58] Original words: *Just so should it be in*

[59] Original words: *that they may be*

[60] Original word: *moved*

[61] Romans 8:14

[62] Original sentence: *As all action is estimable only in proportion to the grandeur and dignity of the efficient principle, this action is incontestably more noble than any other.*

[63] Original sentence: *Actions produced by a divine principle, are divine; but creaturely actions, however good they appear, are only human, or at least virtuous, even when accompanied by grace.*

[64] John 5:26

[65] Original words: *and being communicative of His nature, He desires to bestow it upon man.*

[66] See Romans 6:6, Ephesians 4:22, Colossians 3:9

[67] 2 Corinthians 5:17

[68] Original sentence: *This can only be effected by the consent of the creature; and this concurrence can only be yielded by moderating our own action, that the activity of God may, little by little, be wholly substituted for it.*

[69] Original words: *has exemplified*

[70] Original sentence: *The spirit of man is restless and turbulent; for which reason he does little, though he seems to do a great deal.*

[71] Luke 10:41-42

[72] This is much like Paul said in Galatians 2:20b, "I live; yet not I, but Christ liveth in me: . . ."

[73] Original words: *we are not animated by*

[74] Original word: *expelled*

[75] 1 Corinthians 6:17

[76] Psalm 70:28

[77] Original paragraph: *Divine union has its commencement, its progress, its achievement, and its consummation. It is at first an inclination towards God. When the soul is introverted in the manner before described, it gets within the influence of the central attraction, and acquires an eager desire after union; this is the beginning. It then adheres to Him when it has got nearer and nearer, and finally becomes one, that is, one spirit with Him; and then it is that the spirit which had wandered from God, returns again to its end.*

[78] Original sentence: *Into this way, then, which is the divine motion, and the Spirit of Jesus Christ, we must necessarily enter.*

[79] Romans 8:9

[80] Romans 8:14

[81] Original word: *filiation* — The condition or fact of being the child of a certain parent.

[82] Romans 8:15

[83] Original word: *filiation*

[84] Romans 8:16

[85] Original word: *perceives*

[86] Original word: *testimony*

[87] Original word: *filiation*

[88] Original sentence: *The Spirit of divine action is so necessary in all things, that St. Paul, in the same passage, founds that necessity on our ignorance with respect to what we pray for:*

[89] Romans 8:26

[90] John 11:42

[91] Romans 8:27

[92] Original word: *conformable*

[93] Original word: *superfluous*

[94] Original words: *in the multiplicity of our ways*

[95] Hebrews 4:9-10

[96] Matthew 11:28-30, 1 Peter 5:7

[97] Isaiah 55:2

[98] Original word: *hearkening*

[99] Zechariah 2:13

[100] Original words: *But to engage us still farther to an abandonment without reservation,*

[101] Isaiah 49:15

[102] Original word: *consolation*

[103] Original word: *himself*

22

INTERNAL AND
EXTERNAL ACTS[1]

Distinction between internal and external acts; in this state the acts of the soul are internal, but habitual, continued, direct, lasting, deep, simple, unconscious, and resembling a gentle and perpetual sinking into the ocean of Divinity. A comparison. How to act when we do not sense an [internal] attraction.

There are both[2] external and internal acts. *External* acts are those that appear outwardly, are related to something we can perceive with our senses,[3] and have no moral character except what they derive from the principle [or source] from which they proceed. I am going to speak here only of *internal* acts, those energies of the soul by which it turns internally *toward* some objects and *away from* others.

If while applying myself [internally] to God, I decide to change the nature [or way] of applying myself,

I would by that [action] withdraw from God and turn to created objects, [that is, to things of *self*]—and that [withdrawing from God and turning to *self*] would be small or large depending on the strength of my action. When I am turned toward self and desire to return to God, I must necessarily create an action, [do a specific act], for that purpose—and the more perfect this action is, the more complete will be my conversion, [that is, my turning from *self* to God].[4]

IN THE BEGINNING MANY REPEATED ACTS ARE NECESSARY

Until conversion[5] is complete, many repeated acts [of turning away from *self* to God] are necessary. For some, this conversion is progressive, but with others it is instantaneous.[6] My act [and yours], however, should consist in a continual turning to God, an exertion of every faculty and power of the soul purely for Him, in keeping with[7] the instructions of the son of Sirach: "Re-unite all the motions of thy heart in the holiness of God."[8] Also with the example of David, "I will keep my whole strength for Thee."[9] This is done by earnestly re-entering into ourselves, as Isaiah says, "Return to your heart."[10] It is our heart that has strayed because of sin, and it is *only* our heart that God requires:[11] "My son give Me thine heart, and let thine eyes observe My ways."[12] To give our heart to God is to have the whole energy of our soul always centered in Him, so that we may be made submissive [and quick to comply][13] to His will. Therefore, from the first time we apply ourselves internally to God, we must remain steadily turned to Him.[14]

But [because in the beginning] our spirit is unstable,[15] and our soul is accustomed to turning to external objects, our soul is easily distracted. This evil, however, will be neutralized if at the moment we sense our soul wandering we immediately return its attention to God by a pure act of our will, and instantly put ourselves back in Him. This [latter] state will last as long as the conversion continues—because of the powerful influence of your simple and heartfelt return to God.[16]

REPEATED ACTS CREATE A HABIT

Just as many repeated acts create a habit, the soul develops the habit of conversion—[of continually turning inward to God], and this act that was in the beginning so easily interrupted and distinct—[that is, had to be deliberately performed]—will become a constant [and permanent] experience.[17]

You should not be confused about your soul performing a [simple] act that already exists, and which, in actuality, it could not even attempt to perform [by self-effort] without great difficulty. Sometimes your soul will even withdraw from its now restful state under the pretext of seeking what it already has. That this habit of turning inward has already been formed is confirmed by habitual conversion and habitual love. [In other words, the fact that your soul is continually turning inward and continually expressing love to God is proof that the habit has already been formed and needs no additional acts.] Yet at times your soul will still seek this one act by the use of many other acts, instead of staying attached to God by the one simple act alone.[18]

WANDERING FROM THE INWARD STATE

At times we create with ease many *distinct yet simple* acts, which shows that we have wandered [from our inward state], and by which we re-enter our heart, [and union with God], after having strayed from it. Once we have re-entered, we should remain there in peace. We make a mistake, therefore, in supposing that we must not create acts. We *create them continually*, but they should be in keeping with the degree of our spiritual advancement. [The further you have spiritually advanced, the less there will be of those acts.][19]

The great difficulty with most spiritual people comes from their not clearly understanding this matter. Some acts are *brief and distinct*, while others are *continued*. Some acts are *direct*, while others are *reflective*. Not everyone can create the first, and not everyone is in a [spiritual] state suited to create the others. Acts that are brief and distinct are for those who have strayed, and who require a distinct act in proportion to how far they strayed. If not far, then an act of the most simple kind is sufficient [to return them to their proper inward condition].[20]

THE SOUL COMPLETELY TURNED TOWARD GOD LIVES IN LOVE

By a *continued* act, I mean that whereby the soul is completely[21] turned toward God by a *direct* act, always continuing, and which it does not renew unless it has been interrupted. The soul that is completely turned [toward God] lives in love and remains in it: "he that dwelleth in love dwelleth in God."[22] The soul now exists and rests in this habitual act [of turning toward God]. It is, however, free from idleness, for there is still an *uninterrupted act to maintain*[23] —a *sweet sinking into God,* whose attraction becomes more and more powerful [as the soul draws closer to Him]. Following this powerful attraction, and dwelling in love,[24] the soul sinks continually deeper into that love, maintaining an activity that is infinitely more powerful, energetic, and effective than that by which it first turned inward.[25]

Now the soul that is *profoundly and vigorously active* in this manner, being completely given up to God, does not sense this act. That is because it is direct and not reflective—[inward and not outward]. This is the reason why some who do not express themselves properly say they make no acts. But that is a mistake, for they were never more truly or nobly active. They should say, that *they did not sense their acts, and not that they did not act.* I grant that they do not act of themselves. However, they are drawn [inward] and they follow that attraction. Love is the weight that sinks them. Just as someone falling into an infinite sea would sink from one depth to another throughout all eternity, so they, too, without perceiving their descent, drop with inconceivable swiftness into the deepest depths [of God.][26]

WRONG TO SAY WE DO NOT MAKE ACTS

So it is wrong to say that we do not make acts. Everyone makes acts, but the way they are made is not the same in everyone. The mistake arises from this—all those who know they should act, desire to act in a way that they can *recognize and observe.*[27] But this cannot be—observable acts are for beginners, and there are different [acts] for those in a more advanced [spiritual] state. To stay in observable acts, which are weak and of little profit [to those in an advanced state], is to exclude ourselves from the deeper acts. In the same way, to attempt the deeper acts without having passed through the observable acts [for beginners] is also a great error.[28]

"To everything there is a season."[29] Every [spiritual] state has its beginning, its progress, and its completion—and it is an unhappy mistake to stop in the beginning. There is no art that does not have its [time of] progress. At first, we labor with effort, but ultimately we reap the fruit of our labor.

MOVING A VESSEL AWAY FROM THE DOCKS INTO THE OPEN SEA

When the vessel is in port,[30] the sailors must exert all their strength [on the oars] to move it away from the docks and out into the open sea. Once they are there, however, they can easily turn the vessel in any direction they want to go. In the same way, while your soul remains bound by sin and self, it requires many repeated efforts to set it free. The cables [of sin and self] that hold it must [first] be loosened. Then by strong and vigorous efforts your soul must turn itself inward, pushing off gradually from the old port of *self*. Leaving that behind, it then travels inwardly [to the center of your being], the haven [of rest] it has so much desired.[31]

When the vessel is moved away from the docks and out into the open sea, it gradually leaves the shore behind—and the farther it moves away from the land, the less effort is needed to move it forward. At length the vessel begins to get gently under sail,[32] and now proceeds so swiftly in its course that the oars have become useless and are laid aside. What does the pilot [of the vessel] now have to do? Now he has to do nothing more than spread the sails and hold the rudder.[33]

To spread the sails, is to lay ourselves before God with a prayer of simple explanation [of why we've come before Him], and to be moved [in the prayer] by His Spirit. *To hold the rudder* is to keep our heart from wandering from the true course, recalling it gently, and steering it steadily by the guidance of the Holy Spirit,[34] who gradually gains possession of the heart, just as the breeze gradually fills the sails and moves the vessel. While the winds are favorable, the pilot and the sailors rest from their efforts. Their progress now is swift and sure[35] without the least fatigue! By resting and leaving the vessel to the wind, they make more progress in one hour than they did in several hours by all their previous efforts. And if they now attempt to use the oars, they would only slow the vessel by their useless efforts and greatly tire themselves.

This is our proper inward course. The propelling force of the Holy Spirit moving us inward will advance us further than many repeated acts of self-exertion.[36] Whoever will try this path, will find it the easiest in the world.

HOLDING THE VESSEL STEADY

If the wind is contrary and creates a storm, we must drop the anchor into the sea to hold the vessel steady. This anchor is simply trust in God and hope in His goodness—waiting patiently for the calming of the storm and the return of a favorable wind. David said, "I waited patiently for the LORD; and He inclined unto me, and heard my cry.[37] We must, therefore, be surrendered to the Spirit of God, giving ourselves up completely to His divine guidance.

¹ Original title: *On Inward and Outward Acts*

² Original words: *Acts are distinguished into*

³ Original words: *some sensible object*

⁴ Original paragraph: *If during my application to God, I should form a will to change the nature of my act, I should thereby withdraw myself from God and turn to created objects, and that in a greater or less degree according to the strength of the act: and if, when I am turned towards the creature, I would return to God, I must necessarily form an act for that purpose; and the more perfect this act is, the more complete is the conversion.*

⁵ By *conversion*, Madame Guyon is referring to continually turning away from *self* to God until it becomes an automatic action—a habit.

⁶ Original sentence: *Till conversion is perfected, many reiterated acts are necessary; for it is with some progressive, though with others it is instantaneous.*

⁷ Original words: *agreeable to*

⁸ Apocrypha, Ecclesiasticus 30:24. One translation reads, "Have pity on thy own soul, pleasing God, and contain thyself: gather up thy heart in His holiness: and drive away sadness far from thee.

⁹ Vulgate, Psalm 59:9 — KJV reads, "Because of his strength will I wait upon Thee: for God is my defence."

¹⁰ Vulgate, Isaiah 46:8 — KJV reads, "bring it again to mind."

¹¹ Original sentence: *For we have strayed from our heart by sin, and it is our heart only that God requires*

¹² Proverbs 23:26

¹³ Original word: *conformable*

¹⁴ Original sentence: *We must, therefore, continue invariably turned to God, from our first application to Him.*

¹⁵ Original words: *But the spirit being unstable*

¹⁶ Original paragraph: *This evil, however, will be counteracted if, on perceiving the wandering, we, by a pure act of return to God, instantly replace ourselves in Him; and this act subsists as long as the conversion lasts, by the powerful influence of a simple and unfeigned return to God.*

¹⁷ Original paragraph: *As many reiterated acts form a habit, the soul contracts the habit of conversion; and that act which was before interrupted and distinct becomes habitual.*

¹⁸ Original paragraph: *The soul should not, then, be perplexed about forming an act which already subsists, and which, indeed, it cannot attempt to form without very great difficulty; it even finds that it is withdrawn from its proper state, under pretence of seeking that which is in reality acquired, seeing the habit is already formed, and it is confirmed in habitual conversion and habitual love. It is seeking one act by the help of many, instead of continuing attached to God by one simple act alone.*

¹⁹ Original paragraph: *We may remark, that at times we form with facility many distinct yet simple acts; which shows that we have wandered, and that we re-enter our heart after having strayed from it; yet when we have re-entered, we should remain there in peace. We err, therefore, in supposing that we must not form acts; we form them continually: but let them be conformable to the degree of our spiritual advancement.*

²⁰ Original paragraph: *The great difficulty with most*

spiritual people arises from their not clearly comprehending this matter. Now, some acts are transient and distinct, others are continued, and again, some are direct, and others reflective. All cannot form the first, neither are all in a state suited to form the others. The first are adapted to those who have strayed, and who require a distinct exertion, proportioned to the extent of their deviation; if the latter be inconsiderable, an act of the most simple kind is sufficient.

[21] Original word: *altogether*

[22] 1 John 4:16

[23] Original words: *uninterrupted act subsisting*

[24] Original words: *love and charity* — In the KJV NT, the word charity is used for love.

[25] Original words: *which served to accomplish its first return*

[26] Original sentence: *As one falling into the sea, would sink from one depth to another to all eternity, if the sea were infinite, so they, without perceiving their descent, drop with inconceivable swiftness into the lowest deeps.*

[27] Original words: *are desirous of acting distinguishably and perceptibly;*

[28] Original sentence: *To stop in the former, which are weak and of little profit, is to debar ourselves of the latter; as to attempt the latter without having passed through the former, is a no less considerable error.*

[29] Ecclesiastes 3:1

[30] In Madame Guyon's time there were only sailing vessels, of course, and that's the type of vessel she's referring to in her example.

[31] Psalm 107:30 - Then they are glad because they are quiet; So He guides them to their desired haven. — Original paragraph: *When the vessel is in port, the mariners are obliged to exert all their strength, that they may clear her thence, and put to sea; but they subsequently turn her with facility as they please. In like manner, while the soul remains in sin and the creature, many endeavors are requisite to effect its freedom; the cables which hold it must be loosed, and then by strong and vigorous efforts it gathers itself inward, pushes off gradually from the old port of Self, and, leaving that behind, proceeds to the interior, the haven so much desired.*

[32] Once out in the open seas, the pilot would direct the vessel into a wind that would fill the sails and move the vessel in the direction he wanted it to go.

[33] Original paragraph: *When the vessel is thus started, as she advances on the sea, she leaves the shore behind; and the farther she departs from the land, the less labor is requisite in moving her forward. At length she begins to get gently under sail, and now proceeds so swiftly in her course, that the oars, which are become useless, are laid aside. How is the pilot now employed? he is content with spreading the sails and holding the rudder.*

[34] Psalm 32:8, Isaiah 58:11, John 16:13

[35] Original words: *What progress do they not now secure,*

[36] Original words: *This is our proper course interiorly, and a short time will advance us by the divine impulsion farther than many reiterated acts of self-exertion.*

[37] Psalm 40:1

23

AN EXHORTATION TO CHRISTIAN MINISTERS AND WORKERS[1]

The barrenness of preaching, vice, error, heresies, and all sorts of evils arise from the fact that the people are not instructed in the prayer of the heart—even though the way is surer, easier, and fitter for the simple minded. Exhortation to pastors to set their flocks upon the practice of it, without engaging them in elaborate forms and methods of devotion.

If all who labored for the salvation of sinners[2] sought to reach them *by the heart,* introducing them immediately into prayer and the internal life, numberless and permanent conversions would result. By contrast, there are few and [often] temporary results from labor that is confined to exterior matters, such as burdening new converts with a thousand rules and external exercises instead of teaching them the internal life and giving their whole heart to Christ.[3]

If ministers were careful to instruct their new converts [in this way], every kind of vice would shortly disappear [in them], and they would all become spiritually minded. While shepherds watched their flocks they would have the spirit of the primitive Christians. Farmers at their plows would maintain a blessed conversation with their God. Manufacturers [and factory workers] who exhausted themselves physically with outward labor would be renewed with inward strength.[4] [All would benefit from the internal life with Christ.][5]

A heart gained by Christ is easily corrected

O when once the *heart* is gained [by Christ], how easily is everything else corrected! This is why God requires the *heart* above all things. By this means alone—[by Christ dwelling in the heart][6], we could destroy the dreadful sins that often continue among new converts, such as drinking, lust, resentment, selfishness, anger, unforgiveness.[7] *Jesus Christ* would reign everywhere in peace, and the face of the Church would be renewed throughout.

Loss of internal holiness causes errors

The loss of internal holiness is unquestionably the source of the various errors that have appeared in the Church. All of them would speedily be overthrown [and the Church returned to what Christ intended it to be], if inward devotion was re-established. Errors take possession of no soul except those that are deficient in faith and prayer. If instead of continually debating and arguing with wandering brothers and sisters,[8] we would just teach them to simply *believe* and diligently *pray* we would lead them sweetly back to God.[9]

O how inexpressibly great is the loss sustained by Christians[10] from the neglect of the interior life! And those who are entrusted with the care of souls and have not discovered and communicated to their flock this hidden treasure will have to give an account to Christ![11]

NO DANGER IN THIS METHOD OF PRAYER

Some excuse themselves by saying that there is danger in this way [of praying], or that simple persons are incapable of understanding the things of the Spirit. But the oracles of truth say the opposite:[12] "The Lord loveth those who walk simply."[13] But what danger can there be in walking in the only true way, which is Jesus Christ? [Can there possibly be any danger in] giving ourselves up to Him, fixing our eye continually on Him, placing all our confidence in His grace, and moving [forward] with all the strength of our soul into His purest love?

Far from being *incapable* of this perfection, the *simple* ones are especially qualified to obtain it because of their innocence, humility, and willingness to learn. Also, since they do not analyze and reason everything out, they do not hold stubbornly to their own opinions.[14] Because of that,[15] they submit more freely to the teachings of the Holy Spirit. Others, however,[16] who are cramped and blinded by self-sufficiency, offer much greater resistance to the operations of grace.

GOD GIVES UNDERSTANDING TO THE SIMPLE

We are told in Scripture that "unto the simple, God giveth the understanding of His law."[17] We are also assured, that God loves to communicate with them: "The Lord careth for the simple; I was reduced to extremity and He saved me."[18] Those who have new converts in their care should be careful that they do not prevent them from coming [simply and truly like little children] to Christ.[19] He Himself said to His disciples, "Suffer little children, and forbid them not, to come unto Me: for of such is the kingdom of heaven."[20] It was the effort of the apostles to prevent children from going to our Lord that resulted in[21] this command.

People[22] frequently apply a remedy to the outward body while the disease is in the heart. The cause of our being so unsuccessful in reforming humanity, especially those of the lower classes,[23] is that we begin with external matters. All such efforts do nothing but produce fruit that does not last.[24] But if the *key to the interior* [spiritual life] is given first, the exterior will be naturally and easily reformed.

Teach new converts to seek God in their heart

Now this is very easy. Simply teach new converts[25] to seek God in their heart, to think of Him [continually], to return to Him whenever they find they have wandered from Him, and to do and suffer all things with a single eye to please Him. [When you do this], you lead their soul to the source of all grace, and enable them to find there everything necessary for sanctification.

Teach this way of prayer at once

I therefore beseech all who have the care of souls to teach them this way of prayer at once—for this way *is* Jesus Christ. Indeed, it is He Himself who urges you by all the blood He has shed for those entrusted to you. "Speak to the heart of Jerusalem!"[26] O you dispensers of His grace! preachers of His word! ministers of His sacraments! establish His kingdom!— and that it may indeed be established, make Him *ruler over the heart!* For as it is the heart alone that can oppose His sovereignty. [Therefore], it is by the surrender of the heart that His sovereignty is most highly honored. "Give glory to the holiness of God, and He shall become your sanctification."[27] Compose Bible lessons[28] expressly to teach prayer—and not by reasoning or by method, for the simple are incapable of that. Teach the prayer of the heart, not of the understanding—the prayer of God's Spirit, not of people's invention.[29]

CREATING OBSTACLES FOR BELIEVERS

When you teach believers to pray in *elaborate forms*, and to be highly critical of their own prayers, you create their chief obstacles. The children have been led astray from the best of fathers, [which is what you do] by trying to teach them to pray in a precise and pure language. Go you poor children to your heavenly Father, speak to him in your natural language. Even if your words are rude and barbarous, they are not so to Him. A father is pleased more with hearing words that love and respect have made confused, but which he sees comes from the heart, than he is by a dry and barren speech, no matter how elaborate [and refined] it is. The simple and undisguised emotions of love are infinitely more expressive than all [refined] language and all reasoning.[30]

UNNECESSARY TO TEACH THE ART OF LOVING

People have desired to love [He who is] *Love* by formal rules, and have therefore lost much of that love. O how unnecessary is it to teach the art of loving! The language of love is coarse [and unrefined] to a person who does not love, but is perfectly natural to one who

147

does. The best way to learn how to love God is to love Him. The most ignorant often become the most perfect [in loving God], because they proceed with more warmth and simplicity. The Spirit of God needs none of our arrangements [or elaborate methods of prayer]. When it pleases Him, He turns shepherds into prophets.[31] And instead of excluding any from the temple of prayer, He throws wide the gates so that all may enter. Wisdom is directed to cry aloud in the highways, "Whoso is simple let him turn in hither"[32] To the fools, wisdom says, "Come eat of my bread, and drink of the wine which I have mingled."[33] And does not Jesus Christ Himself say to God, "I thank Thee, O Father, Lord of heaven and earth, because *Thou hast hid these things from the wise and prudent, and hast revealed them unto babes"?*[34]

[1] Original title: *An Exhortation to Ministers*

[2] Original words: *conversion of others*

[3] Madame Guyon was referring particularly to the methods of her church, but even today a major evangelistic organization in the United States admits that less than 10% of those who "accept Christ" at their crusades ever end up as permanent members of any church. They accept and justify that low percentage by quoting Jesus' teaching about the "the sower sows the word" in Mark 4:14-20, where only 1 in 4 yield a crop.

Original sentence: *On the contrary, few and transient fruits must attend that labor which is confined to outward matters, such as burdening the disciple with a thousand precepts for external exercises, instead of leading the soul to Christ by the occupation of the heart in Him.*

[4] 2 Corinthians 4:16

[5] Original paragraph: *If ministers were solicitous thus to instruct their parishioners, shepherds, while they watched their flocks, would have the spirit of the primitive Christians, and the husbandman at the plough maintain a blessed intercourse with his God; the manufacturer, while he exhausted his outward man with labor, would be renewed with inward strength; every species of vice would shortly disappear, and every parishioner become spiritually minded.*

[6] Ephesians 3:14-19

[7] Original words: *prevail among the lower orders, such as drunkenness, blasphemy, lewdness, enmity and theft.* Madame Guyon is speaking here of many who came into her church in her day without true conversion.

[8] Original words: *engaging our wandering brethren in*

constant disputations

[9] James 5:16

[10] Original word: *mankind*

[11] Original sentence: *And what an account will those have to render who are entrusted with the care of souls, and have not discovered and communicated to their flock this hidden treasure!* (See 2 Corinthians 5:10-11)

[12] Original words: *affirm the contrary*

[13] Vulgate, Proverbs 12:22

[14] Original words: *and, as they are not accustomed to reasoning, they are less tenacious of their own opinions.*

[15] Original words: *Even from their want of learning*

[16] Original words: *whereas others*

[17] Vulgate, Psalm 119:130

[18] Vulgate, Psalm 116:6 (KJV: The LORD preserveth the simple: I was brought low, and He helped me.)

[19] Original sentence: *Let spiritual fathers be careful how they prevent their little ones from coming to Christ;*

[20] Matthew 19:14

[21] Original word: *occasioned*

[22] Original word: *Man*

[23] In Madame Guyon's time, the "lower classes" were those who were poor and uneducated, as opposed to the "upper classes" who were affluent and educated to varying degrees.

[24] Original words: *all our labors in this field, do but produce such fruit as endures not;*

[25] Original word: *man*

[26] Vulgate, Isaiah 40:2

[27] Vulgate, Isaiah 8:13 — (KJV: "Sanctify the LORD of hosts Himself; and let Him be your fear, and let him be your dread.") Vulgate rendering of Isaiah 8:13 is much like the KJV rendering of Psalm 29:2—" Give unto the LORD the glory due unto His name; worship the LORD in the beauty of holiness."

[28] Original word: *catechisms*

[29] Original paragraph: *I therefore beseech you all, O ye that have the care of souls, to put them at once into this way, which is Jesus Christ; nay, it is He Himself that conjures you, by all the blood He has shed for those entrusted to you. "Speak to the heart of Jerusalem!" (*Isa. xl. 2, vulg.*) O ye dispensers of His grace! preachers of His word! ministers of His sacraments! establish His kingdom!— and that it may indeed be established, make Him RULER OVER THE HEART! For as it is the heart alone that can oppose His sovereignty, it is by the subjection of the heart that His sovereignty is most highly honored: "Give glory to the holiness of God, and He shall become your sanctification." (*Isa. viii. 13, vulg.*) Compose catechisms expressly to teach prayer, not by reasoning nor by method, for the simple are incapable of that; but to teach the prayer of the heart, not of the understanding; the prayer of God's Spirit, not of man's invention.*

[30] Original paragraph: *Alas! by directing them to pray in elaborate forms, and to be curiously critical therein, you create their chief obstacles. The children have been led astray from the best of fathers, by your endeavoring to teach them too refined a language. Go, then, ye poor children, to your heavenly Father, speak to Him in your natural language; rude and barbarous as it may be, it is not so to Him. A father is better pleased with an*

address which love and respect have made confused, because he sees that it proceeds from the heart, than he is by a dry and barren harangue, though never so elaborate. The simple and undisguised emotions of love are infinitely more expressive than all language, and all reasoning.

[31] 1 Samuel 16:13

[32] Proverbs 9:4 — This verse in Proverbs is not intended for the way Madame Guyon is using it, but out of context it is appropriate for her use.

[33] Proverbs 9:5 — Above comment applies here also.

[34] Matthew 11:25

24

THE EASY WAY TO UNION WITH GOD[1]

It is impossible to achieve union with God by meditation alone, or by your affections or devotion, no matter how [spiritually] enlightened they may be. There are many reasons for this—here are the major ones.

NO ONE SHALL SEE GOD AND LIVE

According to Scripture, "no man shall see God and live."[2] Now all the activity of intellectual, reasoning, prayer, and even active contemplation, that are considered to be the ultimate in prayer—[requiring nothing more], and not merely a preparation for true passive prayer, are still *living* exercises—[that is, it is still *you* doing the praying]. [Because it is *you* praying], you cannot see God—that is, be united with Him [that way]. All that is of yourself, no matter how noble or exalted, must first be destroyed.[3]

Silence in heaven

The apostle John says that "there was silence in heaven."[4] Now heaven represents the substance and center of the soul, where everything must be hushed to silence when the majesty of God appears. All *self*-efforts—indeed, the very existence of *self* [in the soul]—must be eliminated. All the evil in humanity comes from self-appropriation, [seizing for oneself all it can]—this is the source of humanity's evil nature. [This can be easily seen in that] the purity of a soul increases in direct proportion to the amount of selfhood—[self-centeredness]—that it loses. Consequently, after the soul has departed from self-centeredness, which caused an obvious difference between it and God, and acquired the purity and innocence [that results], what was a fault while the soul lived in self-appropriation is no longer a fault.[5]

Uniting God's purity and our impurity

To unite two things so opposite as the purity of God and our impurity, the simplicity, [or oneness], of God and our multiplicity, [or excessive ways], much more is needed than *our* efforts. Nothing less than an effective operation of the Almighty can ever accomplish this. Two things cannot become one until they have some relation or similarity, just as dross, the impurity from a metal, cannot be united with the purity of gold.

What, then, does God do? He sends His own wisdom before Him [to accomplish the work in us]. [It is like the] fire that will be sent upon the earth to destroy all that is impure. Nothing will be able to resist the power of that fire, it will consume everything.[6] In the same way, God's wisdom destroys all the impurities within our soul in order to prepare it for divine union.[7]

154

THE IMPURITIES THAT ARE FATAL TO UNION WITH GOD

The impurities that are so fatal to union are *self-appropriation* and *activity*. *Self-appropriation* because it is the source and fountain of all that defilement that can never be united to God's purity. The rays of the sun may shine upon mire, but they can never be united with it. *Activity* because God exists in an infinite stillness, and for the soul to be united to Him it must participate in His stillness. Otherwise, the opposition between stillness and activity would prevent assimilation [of your soul by God].[8]

Our soul, therefore, can never arrive at divine union until we put our will to rest—[stop all *self*-activity]. Further, it can never become one with God until it is re-established in complete rest at its center, and returned to the purity it had when it was first created.[9]

GOD PURIFIES OUR SOUL BY HIS WISDOM

God purifies the soul by His wisdom, as refiners purify metals in the furnace. Gold cannot be purified except by fire, which gradually consumes all dirt and foreign material and separates them from the metal. Those things cannot be made fit for use by changing them into gold, [that is obviously impossible]. So the mass of material must be melted and dissolved by the force of fire to separate every particle of dirt and foreign matter from the gold. It must be cast into the fire again and again until the gold has lost every trace of pollution, and there is no possibility of its being further purified.[10]

The goldsmith cannot now discover any impure[11] mixture because of the gold's perfect purity and simplicity. The fire no longer touches it, and if it remained for a hundred years in the furnace, its purity would not be increased or its substance diminished. It is now fit for the most exquisite workmanship, and if this gold ever seems hidden or defiled after that, it is nothing more than an accidental impurity caused by contact with some foreign body, and is only superficial. This [minor and temporary] impurity does not hinder its use [by God], and is widely different from the former corruption that was hidden in the ground of its nature and identified with it.[12] There are some uninstructed people, however, who upon seeing the pure gold stained by some external pollution would be inclined to prefer an impure and gross metal that appeared superficially bright and polished.[13] [[14]]

PURE AND IMPURE GOLD ARE NOT MINGLED

Also, pure gold and impure gold are not mingled. Before they can be united, they must be equally refined. The goldsmith cannot mix dross[15] and gold. What will he do, then? He will purge out the dross with fire so that the inferior may become as pure as the other— then they can be united. This is what the apostle Paul means when he declares that, "the fire shall try every man's work of what sort it is"[16] To that he adds, "If any man's work shall be burnt, he shall suffer loss: but he himself shall be saved; yet so as by fire."[17] He here indicates that there are works so degraded by impure mixtures, that though the mercy of God accepts the person, that person must pass through the fire to be purged from *self*. It is in this sense that God is said to examine and judge our righteousness. [As it is written], "by the deeds of the law there shall no flesh be justified in His sight" . . . but only by "the righteousness of God which is by faith in Jesus Christ."[18]

Thus we can see that the divine justice and wisdom must be like a pitiless and devouring fire and destroy everything that is earthly, sensual, and carnal, and all self-activity, before the soul can be united to its God. Now this can never be accomplished by our activity. In fact, we always submit to it with reluctance, because, as I have said, we are so in love with[19] *self* and so fearful of its destruction, that if God does not act upon us powerfully and with authority we would never consent.

DOES GOD ROB US OF OUR FREE WILL?

You may object here and say that since God never robs us of our free will we can always resist the divine operations. Therefore, I am mistaken in saying *God acts absolutely and without our consent.*

Let me, however, explain. By your giving a *passive consent,* God may assume full control and complete guidance [of your soul] without doing it against your will. That is because when you were first converted to Christ, you made an unreserved surrender of yourself to all that God wills of you, by you, [or through you].[20] By so doing, you gave your active consent to whatever God might afterwards require [of you]. However, when God begins to burn, destroy, and purify, your soul might not realize that these operations are intended for its good, but rather believe the opposite. Just as gold at first seems rather to blacken than brighten in the fire, so your soul thinks that its purity is lost. So much so, that if an *active and unreserved* consent were then required, your soul would hardly be able to give it, and would often withhold it. All your soul can do, therefore, is remain firm in passive consent, enduring as patiently as possible all these divine operations, which it is not able to prevent [anyway, and should not even desire to try].[21]

Our soul purified from all self-originating activities

It is by this action of God that your soul is purified from all its self-originating, distinct, perceptible, and multiple activities that constitute a great [opposing] difference between it and God. Gradually your soul is changed to *conform* to God's will, and then changed so that its will and God's will are *uniform*—[that is, the same]. When this occurs, your ability to remain passive before God is elevated, ennobled, and enlarged. Since this is done in a secret and hidden manner, it is called *mystical* [by many]. Nevertheless, the soul must agree to all these [hidden] operations of God, but it must do so passively. It is true, indeed, that in the beginning [of these operations] its activity is needed. As the divine operations become stronger, however, the soul must gradually cease any activity. It must simply yield itself to the impulses of the divine Spirit until it is wholly absorbed in Him. This [final] process takes a long time— [it is not accomplished in a few weeks or even a few months].[22]

I do not say, then, as some have supposed, that there is no need of [any] *activity*. On the contrary, activity is the gate [through which the soul must enter]. We should not, however, remain at the gate, since we should be moving toward ultimate perfection, which is not possible unless the first helps are laid aside. Although they may have been necessary at the entrance to this path, after that they become greatly detrimental to those who hold stubbornly to them, preventing them from ever reaching the end.[23] It was for this reason that the apostle Paul wrote, "Forgetting those things which are behind, and reaching forth unto those things which are before,

I press toward the mark for the prize of the high calling of God in Christ Jesus."[24]

TRAVELERS ON A LONG JOURNEY

Would you not say that travelers who had started a long journey are somewhat foolish if they make the first inn where they stay their permanent home, because they had been told that many travelers had come that way, that some had lodged there, and that the owners of the inn lived there? All that I wish, then, is that those [who start this journey] press on toward the end, taking the shortest and easiest path and not stopping at the first stage. Let them follow the counsel and example of the apostle Paul and allow themselves *to be led by the Spirit of God*,[25] who will unerringly conduct them to the end for which they were created—the enjoyment of God.[26]

It is strange that while we confess that the enjoyment of God is the only purpose for which we were created, and that every soul that does not in this life achieve divine union and the purity of its original creation[27] can only be saved as by fire,[28] we dread and avoid the process. It is as if we think that this process is the cause of evil and imperfection in this present life. But the purpose [of this present life] is to [begin] to produce the perfect of glory in the life to come—[a foretaste here of what we shall have there].[29]

GOD IS THE SUPREME GOOD

Surely no one can be ignorant of the fact that God is the Supreme Good, and that ultimate happiness, the highest state of contentment and joy, is union with Him. Nor can any be ignorant of the fact that saints differ in glory, according to how perfect their union is with God.

159

Also, that the soul—[which is to say, the person]—cannot achieve this union by the mere activity of its own powers. It is God who must communicate Himself to the soul, and He does it in direct proportion to how great, noble, and extensive the soul's passive capacity is—[that is, its ability to remain passive while God performs the work of union]. We can only be united to God in simplicity and passivity, and since this union is blessing itself, the way that leads us in this passivity cannot be evil—it can only be the most free from danger and the best.[30]

THIS WAY IS NOT *DANGEROUS*

Would Jesus Christ have made this the most perfect and necessary of all ways, had it been so? No! All can travel it. And since all are called to happiness, all are likewise called to the enjoyment of God, both in this life and the next, for that *alone* is [true] happiness. I say the enjoyment of God *Himself*, and not of His gifts. The gifts do not constitute ultimate happiness, since they cannot fully satisfy the soul. The soul is so noble and so great that the most exalted gifts of God cannot make it happy, unless the Giver [of the gifts] also gives Himself. Now God's total desire is to give Himself to every soul, and He does in proportion to the capacity of each soul to receive Him. But, alas, how reluctantly God's children are to allow themselves to be drawn in to God—how fearful they are to prepare for divine union![31]

WE CANNOT PUT OURSELVES IN UNION WITH GOD

Some say that we *must not put ourselves into this state [of union with God]*. I agree, but I say also that no creature could ever do it. It would not be possible for any to unite themselves to God by *all* their own efforts. It is He alone who must do it. It is altogether useless, therefore, to exclaim against those who [claim they] are self-united, since such a thing is impossible.

They also say that *some may pretend to have attained this state.* None can any more pretend this than a person who is starving to death can pretend, for any length of time at least, to be full and satisfied. Some wish or word, some sigh or sign, will inevitably escape from anyone so pretending, and betray [the fact] that they are far from being satisfied.

NONE CAN ACHIEVE UNION BY THEIR OWN EFFORTS

Since then none can achieve union with God[32] by their own efforts, we do not pretend to introduce any into it, but *only to point out the way that leads to it.* We also beseech everyone [who starts this journey] not *to become attached to the accommodations—those beginning external activities—on the road. They must all be left behind when the signal* [to move on] *is given* [by the Holy Spirit]. The experienced teacher knows this, points [the beginning travelers] to the water of life, and gives them whatever aid [is needed] to obtain it. Would it not be extremely cruel to show a spring to thirsty travelers, then hold them back so they could not reach it, and let them die of thirst?

This is just what is done every day. So let us all agree in the *way,* even as we all agree [that God's desire] in the *end* [is union with Him], which is obvious and uncontestable. The way has its beginning, progress, and end—its consummation. The nearer we come to the end, the further we leave the beginning behind us. It is only by leaving the one that we can arrive at the other. You cannot get from the place where you start to a distant

161

place without traveling over the road in between. So if the end is good, holy, and necessary, and the starting place is also good, why should the way by which you must travel—the direct road leading from the one to the other—be evil?[33]

THE BLINDNESS OF HUMAN PRIDE

O the blindness of the greater part of humanity, who pride themselves on science and wisdom! How true is it, O my God, "that thou hast hid these things from the wise and prudent, and hast revealed them unto babes!"[34]

[1] Original title: *On the Passive Way to Divine Union*

[2] Slight paraphrase of Exodus 33:20.

[3] Original sentences: *Now all the exercises of discursive prayer, and even of active contemplation, regarded as an end, and not as a mere preparative to that which is passive, are still living exercises, by which we cannot see God; that is to say, be united with him. All that is of man and of his doing, be it never so noble, never so exalted, must first be destroyed.*

[4] Revelation 8:1

[5] Original sentence: *All the efforts, nay, the very existence, of self, must be destroyed; because nothing is opposite to God, but self, and all the malignity of man is in self-appropriation, as the source of its evil nature; insomuch that the purity of a soul increases in proportion as it loses this self-hood; and that which was a fault while the soul lived in self-appropriation, is no longer such, after it has acquired purity and innocence, by departing from that self-hood, which caused the dissimilitude between it and God.*

[6] 2 Peter 3:7, 10

[7] Original sentence: *He sends His own Wisdom before Him, as fire shall be sent upon the earth, to destroy by its activity all that is impure; and as nothing can resist the power of that fire, but it consumes everything, so this Wisdom destroys all the impurities of the creature, in order to dispose it for divine union.*

[8] Original paragraph: *The impurity which is so fatal to union consists in self-appropriation and activity. Self-appropriation; because it is the source and fountain of all that defilement which can never be allied to essential purity; as the rays of the sun may shine, indeed, upon*

mire, but can never be united with it. Activity; for God being in an infinite stillness, the soul, in order to be united to Him, must participate of His stillness, else the contrariety between stillness and activity would prevent assimilation.

[9] Original sentence: *Therefore, the soul can never arrive at divine union but in the rest of its will; nor can it ever become one with God, but by being re-established in central rest and in the purity of its first creation.*

[10] Original sentence: *It is not sufficient to fit it for use that the earthy part should be changed into gold; it must then be melted and dissolved by the force of fire, to separate from the mass every drossy or alien particle; and must be again and again cast into the furnace, until it has lost every trace of pollution, and every possibility of being farther purified.*

[11] Original word: *adulterate*

[12] Original sentence: *The fire no longer touches it; and were it to remain an age in the furnace, its spotlessness would not be increased, nor its substance diminished. It is then fit for the most exquisite workmanship, and if, thereafter, this gold seem obscured or defiled, it is nothing more than an accidental impurity occasioned by the contact of some foreign body, and is only superficial; it is no hinderance to its employment, and is widely different from its former debasement, which was hidden in the ground of its nature, and, as it were, identified with it.*

[13] Original sentence: *Those, however, who are uninstructed, beholding the pure gold sullied by some external pollution, would be disposed to prefer an impure and gross metal, that appeared superficially bright and polished.*

[14] Comment by Madame Guyon in a defense she wrote of her book: "God knows that (in speaking of the superficial impurity) I had only reference to certain defects which are exterior and entirely natural, and which are left by God in the greatest saints to keep them from pride, and the sight of others, who judge only from the outward appearance, to preserve them from corruption, and hide them in the secret of His presence. (Psalm 31:20.) At the time I wrote, I had heard no mention of the perversions subsequently spoken of that those in union with God might sin and yet remain united to Him, and, as such an idea had not once occurred to me, I never imagined that it was possible for any one to draw such inferences from a simple illustration."

[15] *dross*: a waste product or an impurity, especially an oxide, formed on the surface of molten metal.

[16] 1 Corinthians 3:13

[17] 1 Corinthians 3:15

[18] Romans 3:20a, 22a

[19] Original word: *enamored*

[20] Philippians 2:13

[21] Original paragraph: *Let me, however, explain. By man's giving a passive consent, God, without usurpation, may assume full power and an entire guidance; for having, in the beginning of his conversion, made an unreserved surrender of himself to all that God wills of him or by him, he thereby gave an active consent to whatever God might afterwards require. But when God begins to burn, destroy, and purify, the soul does not perceive that these operations are intended for its good, but rather supposes the contrary; and, as the gold at first seems rather to*

blacken than brighten in the fire, so it conceives that its purity is lost; insomuch, that if an active and explicit consent were then required, the soul could scarcely give it, nay would often withhold it. All it does is to remain firm in its passive consent, enduring as patiently as possible all these divine operations, which it is neither able nor desirous to obstruct.

[22] Original paragraph: *In this manner, therefore, the soul is purified from all its self-originated, distinct, perceptible, and multiplied operations, which constitute a great dissimilitude between it and God; it is rendered by degrees conform, and then uniform; and the passive capacity of the creature is elevated, ennobled, and enlarged, though in a secret and hidden manner, hence called mystical; but in all these operations the soul must concur passively. It is true, indeed, that in the beginning its activity is requisite; from which, however, as the divine operations become stronger, it must gradually cease; yielding itself up to the impulses of the divine Spirit, till it is wholly absorbed in Him. But this is a process which lasts a long time.*

[23] Original sentences: *We do not, then, say, as some have supposed, that there is no need of* activity; *since, on the contrary, it is the gate; at which, however,* we should not always tarry, *since we ought to tend towards ultimate perfection, which is impracticable except the first helps are laid aside; for however necessary they may have been at the entrance of the road, they afterwards become greatly detrimental to those who adhere to them obstinately, preventing them from ever attaining the end.*

[24] Philippians 3:13-14

[25] Romans 8:14

[26] Original paragraph: *Would you not say that he had lost his senses, who, having undertaken a journey, should fix his abode at the first inn, because he had been told that many travellers had come that way, that some had lodged there, and that the masters of the house dwelt there? All that we wish, then, is, that souls would press toward the end, taking the shortest and easiest road, and not stopping at the first stage. Let them follow the counsel and example of St. Paul, and suffer themselves to be led by the Spirit of God, (Rom. viii. 14,) which will infallibly conduct them to the end of their creation, the enjoyment of God.*

[27] Hebrews 14:14, 1 Peter 1:16

[28] 1 Corinthians 3:15

[29] 2 Corinthians 5:5, Hebrews 6:4

Original paragraph: *But while we confess that the enjoyment of God is the end for which alone we were created, and that every soul that does not attain divine union and the purity of its creation in this life, can only be saved as by fire, how strange it is, that we should dread and avoid the process; as if that could be the cause of evil and imperfection in the present life, which is to produce the perfection of glory in the life to come.*

[30] Original paragraph: *None can be ignorant that God is the Supreme Good; that essential blessedness consists in union with Him; that the saints differ in glory, according as the union is more or less perfect; and that the soul cannot attain this union by the mere activity of its own powers, since God communicates Himself to the soul, in proportion as its passive capacity is great, noble and extensive. We can only be united to*

God in simplicity and passivity, and as this union is beatitude itself, the way that leads us in this passivity cannot be evil, but must be the most free from danger, and the best.

[31] Original sentences: *I say the enjoyment of God Himself, and not of His gifts; these latter do not constitute essential beatitude, as they cannot fully content the soul; it is so noble and so great, that the most exalted gifts of God cannot make it happy, unless the Giver also bestows Himself. Now the whole desire of the Divine Being is to give Himself to every creature, according to the capacity with which it is endowed; and yet, alas! how reluctantly man suffers himself to be drawn to God! how fearful is he to prepare for divine union!*

[32] Original words: *this end*

[33] Original paragraph: *Let us all agree in the WAY, as we all agree in the end, which is evident and incontrovertible. The WAY has its beginning, progress, and termination; and the nearer we approach the consummation, the farther is the beginning behind us; it is only by leaving the one, that we can arrive at the other. You cannot get from the entrance to a distant place, without passing over the intermediate space, and, if the end be good, holy, and necessary, and the entrance also good, why should the necessary passage, the direct road leading from the one to the other, be evil?*

[34] Luke 10:21

Book 2

The Way and Results of Union with God

And the glory which Thou gavest me I have given them; that they may be one, even as We are one, I in them, and Thou in Me, that they may be made perfect in one. [1]

PART I

THE WAY OF UNION
WITH GOD

THE FIRST STAGE:[2] CONVERSION

The first stage is the return of your soul[3] to God [when you receive Jesus Christ as your Lord and Savior]. Being truly converted, it begins to live by means of His grace.

THE SECOND STAGE: THE EFFECTIVE TOUCH OF GOD IN THE WILL[4]

Your soul then receives *an effective touch of God* that invites it to withdraw inward, and teaches it that God is within you and so must be sought there—that He [in Christ] is present in your heart,[5] and must be enjoyed there.

Discovering this in the beginning of your [Christian] walk is a source of very great joy to your soul, as it is a foretaste or pledge of happiness to come.

[So from the beginning],[6] the road your soul is to pursue is opened to it and is shown to be that of the *inward life*. This knowledge is most wonderful, since it is the fountain of all the [blessings and] happiness of your soul, and the solid foundation of [your] inward progress. Those who turn toward God merely through their intellect, even though they enjoy something of spiritual meditation, can never enter into intimate union [with God] unless they quit that path and enter into this way of God's inward touch [on their soul]. For all of God's work is done in our will.[7]

WALKING IN BLIND ABANDONMENT

Those who are led in this way, even though they follow by a blind abandonment [to Him], develop a sweet knowledge [of God]. They never walk by the light of their intellect like the former do. Those receive distinct lights to guide them, and having a clear view of the road they never enter those impenetrable areas of God's hidden will that are reserved for the latter—[those who are led inwardly]. The walk of the former is determined by the evidence they receive from their illuminations,[8] assisted by their reason, and they do well. The latter, however, are destined to pursue blindly an unknown course, which, nevertheless, appears perfectly natural to them, although they seem obliged to feel their way. But they walk with more certainty than the others, who are subject to be misled by their intellectual revelations. That is because the latter are guided by God's supreme will, which leads them wherever and however *He* desires. In addition, all of God's more immediate operations are performed in the center of their soul. That is, in the three powers—spirit, soul, and body, which are gathered into one and absorbed

172

into His will. They then follow by imperceptible degrees the path prescribed for them by that touch [of God] that I spoke of before.[9]

THE WAY OF FAITH

These who follow the inward path are the ones who pursue the *way of faith* and *absolute abandonment.* They have neither desire nor freedom to pursue any other path—all else stifles[10] and embarrasses them. They live in greater [intellectual and emotional] dryness[11] than the others, for since there is nothing distinct to which their minds are attached, their thoughts often wander and have nothing to hold[12] them. Also, since there are differences in souls—[that is, in personalities], some being highly emotional and some being less,[13] so it is with those who are led by [God's] will. The emotional souls have stronger feelings but less solid achievement, and should restrain their too eager temperament and allow their emotions to pass, even when they seem [to be] burning with love. The less emotional souls seem harder and more insensitive and unresponsive, and their behavior appears altogether natural [rather than spiritual]. Nevertheless, there is a delicate something in the depth of [God's] will [within them]—His inner touch—that serves to nourish them. [This delicate something] is, as it were, the center and heart of what the others experience in their minds and emotions— [their thoughts and feelings].[14]

Still, since this support—[this inner nourishment]—is extremely delicate, it frequently becomes imperceptible and is hidden by the slightest thing. This gives rise to great suffering, especially in times of tribulation and temptation. For in the same way that the enjoyment and support are delicate and

173

concealed, the person's will shares the same character to a high degree, so that such people do not have strong wills. Their state is more indifferent and unemotional, and their way steadier [than those with strong wills]. But this does not keep them from having as severe and even more serious trouble than others. For nothing is done in them by impulse, everything takes place, as it were, naturally, and their feeble wills cannot make headway against their foes. Their devotion and faithfulness, however, often excels that of the others. Notice the striking difference between Peter and John. One seems to be overflowing with extraordinary zeal, and falls away at the voice of a maid-servant. The other makes no external manifestation—[on the outside seems unconcerned about all that is happening], and remains faithful unto the end.

You will ask me, then, if these souls are not urged on by any strong influence but walk in blindness, do they do the will of God? [Indeed] they do, more truly [than others], although they have no distinct assurance of it. God's will is engraved in indelible characters on their heart,[15] so that they perform with an abandonment that is indifferent and unforceful,[16] and yet firm and indestructible, what others accomplish who are drawn by intellectual and emotional pleasure.[17]

INFLUENCE OF GOD'S DIVINE TOUCH

Thus they go on under the influence of this divine touch [of God] from one degree to another [and higher degree]. They do it by a faith they can sometimes feel and sometimes cannot,[18] and experience constant alternations of dryness[19] and enjoyment of the presence of God. [During this process,] they discover that the enjoyment becomes continually deeper and less perceptible, and thus more delicate and internal. They discover, too, that in the midst of their dryness, and without any distinct light,[20] they are not the less enlightened, for this stage is full of light[21] in itself, though [it often appears] dark to the person that is in it. This is so true that they find themselves more acquainted with the truth—I mean that truth [that is] implanted in their heart,[22] and which causes [them to] yield everything to the will of God. God's divine will becomes increasingly familiar to them, and they are enabled[23] to penetrate a thousand mysteries that never could have been discovered by the light of [their] reason and knowledge. Without being aware of it, they are[24] gradually preparing for the states that are to follow.

TRIALS OF THE SECOND STAGE

The trials of this [second] stage are alternations of dryness and easiness [of prayer]. The former purified the attachment or tendency and natural desire[25] that we have for the enjoyment of God. So that the whole of this stage[26] is passed in alternating[27] enjoyment, dryness, and easiness, without any intermixture of temptations, except very short-lived[28] ones or certain faults. [That is because] in every stage, from the beginning onward, the faults of nature are much more liable to overtake us in times of dryness than in seasons of internal joy, when the anointing[29] of grace keeps us safe[30] from a thousand evils. In all the preceding stages thus far, the soul is engaged in combating its evil habits, and in trying[31] to overcome them by all sorts of painful self-denial.

In the beginning, when God turned the soul's look inward, He so influenced it against itself that it was obliged to cut off all its enjoyments, even the most innocent, and to load itself with every kind of affliction. God gives no relief[32] to some in this regard until the natural life,[33]—that is, [the life] of the external senses as manifested in appetites, likes, and dislikes—is wholly destroyed.

DESTRUCTION OF THE APPETITES AND DISLIKES

This destruction of the appetites and dislikes[34] of [anything of] the external senses, belongs to the second stage, which I have called, "The Effective Touch of God in the Will." In this stage,[35] the highest and greatest virtue is practiced, especially when the inward drawing is strong and active and the anointing very delicious [to the soul]. For there is no sort of spiritual method that God does not use in the soul[36] to enable it to conquer and overcome *self* in everything. By this constant action, along with the gracious anointing mentioned before,[37] the Spirit gets the upper hand of nature, and the external life[38] comes under subjection [to the Spirit] without resistance. There is, then, no further trouble from this source, any more than if all external feeling had been taken away. This stage is [often] mistaken by those who are only a little enlightened for a condition in which *self* is dead[39]—[but they are far wrong.] It is, indeed, the death of the [external] senses, but there is yet a long way to the Spirit's full control of the soul.[40]

THE THIRD STAGE: PASSIVITY AND INTERNAL SACRIFICE

When we have for some time enjoyed the rest of a victory that has cost us so much trouble [to obtain], and suppose ourselves forever relieved from an enemy whose entire power has been destroyed, we enter into the third stage. This one immediately follows the second stage,[41] which is a way of faith more or less agreeable, according to the [difficulties encountered in that] stage.

As I have stated, [during the second stage] we enter into a condition of alternate dryness and easiness [of prayer]. During the dryness the soul perceives certain external weaknesses, natural defects, which, although slight, take it by surprise. It feels, too, that the strength it had received for the struggle is dying away. This is caused by the loss of our active, inward, power. For although the soul [that is] in the second stage imagines itself to be in silence before God, it is not entirely so. It does not speak, indeed, either in heart or by mouth, but it is in an active striving after God and constantly out-breathing love. Consequently, being the subject of the most powerful love activity, exerted by the Divine Love toward Himself, it is continually leaping, as it were, toward its object—[God]. This activity is accompanied by a delightful and almost constant peace. Since it is from this activity of love that we acquire the strength to overcome nature, it is in the second stage that we practice the greatest virtues and most severe self-denial.[42]

LOVE ACTIVITY REPLACED BY LOVE PASSIVITY

But [as we begin to enter the third stage], this love activity begins to decay and is replaced by a *love passivity*, and as it does our strength to resist [our faults and weaknesses] lessens, also. As this stage advances, and the soul becomes more and more passive, it becomes more and more powerless in combat. We become weaker within as God becomes stronger. Some consider this impossibility of resistance as a great temptation, but they do not see that all our labor, aided and assisted by grace, can only accomplish the conquest of our *external* senses. Once conquered, God takes gradual possession of us internally—[our soul], and becomes

Himself our purifier. And just as He required all our watchfulness while He continued us in a love-activity, so He now requires all our trust to let Him work while He begins to make Himself Lord [externally and internally] by the subjection of our flesh to the Spirit.[43]

It must be noted[44] that all our external perfection depends upon and must follow the internal [perfection]. Therefore, when we are [outwardly] engaged in *active* devotion, however simple, we are [just as] actively and simply engaged against ourselves—[that is, against our inward spiritual progress].

THIRD STAGE DESTROYS INWARD SELF-ACTIVITIES OF THE SOUL

The second degree, therefore, accomplishes the destruction of the [activities of the] outward senses—[those of the flesh], and the third stage [accomplishes the destruction] of the inward [self-activities of the soul]. This is brought about by means of the *love passivity.* But now that God is working internally, He seems to neglect the external, and so the reappearance of [our] defects that we thought were gone—although then only appear in times of dryness.[45]

The nearer we approach the end of the third stage, the longer and more frequent are our times of dryness, and the greater our weakness. This is a purification that serves to destroy our internal feelings, as the love activity put an end to our external [senses]. In each stage, there are alternations of dryness and enjoyment. The dryness serves as a purifier of the joy that is to follow, though it is always painful because of its barrenness and weakness. As soon as we stop practicing self-denials of our own design because of our inability to practice them, those of God take their place. He dispenses these crosses in keeping with the degree [of our spiritual progress].[46] These are not chosen by the soul, however. The soul is guided internally by God and receives whatever crosses He appoints.

THE FOURTH STAGE: NAKED FAITH

The fourth stage is *naked faith*. In this stage we have nothing but internal and external desolation,[47] for the external always follows the internal.

Every stage has its beginning, progress, and completion.

All that has been granted and obtained before this with so much effort is now gradually taken away.

This degree is the longest, and only ends with total death [to *self*—that is,] if the soul is willing to be so desolated—[so barren and distressed]—as to die wholly to self. For there is an infinite number of souls that never pass the first stage, and of those who reach the fourth stage there are *very few* in whom its perfect work is [ever completely] accomplished.

This desolation occurs quite violently in some,[48] and although they suffer more distress than others, yet they have less reason to complain, for the very severity of their affliction is a sort of consolation. There are others who experience only a weakness and a kind of disgust for everything, which gives them a feeling[49] of being a failure in [their Christian] duty and unwilling to obey [God].

DEPRIVED OF VOLUNTARY WORKS

In this stage, we are first deprived of our voluntary works, and become unable to do what we did in the preceding stages. As this increases, we begin to feel a general inability in respect to everything, which, instead of lessening, increases day by day. This weakness and inability gradually takes possession of us, and we enter upon a condition in which we say, "For that which I do, I allow not: for what I would, that do I not; but what I hate, that do I."[50]

After being deprived of all internal and external things that are not essential, the work begins upon those that are. Now the moral excellence that becomes us as a Christian, and about which we are often complacent, disappears—and as it does, our internal spiritual delight and strong support is removed to the same degree. As this support becomes weaker and more difficult to detect, the more noticeable becomes its loss. It must be said, however, that there is no loss except to our own consciousness—[that is, it seems to us that we have lost all spiritual support, but we really have not]. It still exists in our soul, but is undetectable and without apparent action. If it were not hidden, the death and loss of *self* could not be accomplished. So our spiritual support retreats within us, and shuts itself up so closely that our soul is no longer aware of its presence.[51]

WHY DOES GOD TAKE THIS WAY INTO UNION?

Do you ask why God takes this way to bring us into union with Himself? The whole object of this way so far has been to cause the soul to pass from its variety of ways to a conscious single way—one that can still be perceived by the external senses, and then to an unconscious single way—one that cannot be perceived by the senses. The general delight of this latter way is much less attractive than the others. God's way of working is vigorous in the beginning and introduces the soul into the single way that can still be perceived by the senses, and which is a purer and less exquisite pleasure than the initial variety of the soul's ways. Then the soul travels from the perceived single way into the unperceived single way, and from there into faith, which is sustained and worked by love.[52] Thus the soul passes in this way from the sensible to the spiritual, and from the spiritual to naked faith. This causes us to be dead to all spiritual experiences, and makes us die to ourselves and pass into God, so that we may live henceforth from the life of God only.[53]

In the economy[54] of God's grace, then, we begin with sensible[55] things, continue with those that are spiritual, and end by leading the soul gradually into its center, and uniting it with God.

The more deeply our imperceptible [spiritual] support retreats, the more it knits the soul together, so that it cannot continue to multiply itself among a thousand things that it can no longer affect or even perceive. Now being entirely stripped, it is gradually obliged to desert even itself.

SOUL STRIPPED WITHOUT MERCY

The soul, therefore, is stripped without mercy, equally and at the same time of everything both internally and externally. But what is worst of all, it is delivered over to temptations. And the more fully it is given up to temptation, the more completely it is deprived of strength to resist them externally. So it is weakened still further at the very time when it is subjected to more violent attacks. Finally, its internal support is [completely] removed. [While it was available, that internal support] served as the soul's refuge and asylum, but its removal is an evidence of the goodness of God, and of His faithfulness to Himself.[56]

[We may liken it to] a man pursued by a powerful enemy. He fights and defends himself as well as he is able, always contriving, however, to get nearer and nearer to a stronghold of safety. But the longer he fights the weaker he becomes, while the strength of his opponent is constantly increasing. What shall he do? He will gain the portal of the stronghold as skillfully as he can, for there he will find abundant aid. On reaching it, however, he sees that it is closed, and finds that far from giving him any assistance, the keepers have barricaded every loophole of refuge. He [now has nothing he can do but surrender himself] into the hands of his powerful enemy. [When he does,] he realizes [that though he surrendered because he was] defenseless and in despair, he has surrendered himself to his best and truest friend.

Understand, then, that this fourth stage includes all these things—the loss of every good [thing], the accumulation of all sorts of weaknesses, no power[57] to defend, no interior asylum, and God Himself often appears angry [at you]. Then to crown it all—temptations.

WILL BECOMES WEAKER AND WEAKER

I think I hear you now say, "I would submit to all this willingly, providing I might be sure that my will was not in harmony with the evils of the flesh and the weaknesses of the senses." Ah! you would be very happy [if that was the way it was], but that cannot be. In the degree that you become weaker and destitute of every operation and activity of love, however insignificant, your will, which was founded in the strength [and energy] of love, becomes weaker day by day, and gradual disappears. Having disappeared, it is certain that your will takes no part in anything that is happening in your [soul], but is separate—[isolated from it]. Since your will does not [now] manifest itself anywhere by any sign, it gives no assured support to your soul. On the contrary, since your soul no longer finds the will in an attitude of resistance [to anything], it believes that it is consenting to everything, and that it has joined in with the animal will—the will of your flesh, which is the only one perceptible.

You will, perhaps, remind me that I stated before that in the first contest of love-activity, the flesh and the senses had become, as it were, extinguished and subdued. It is true. But *self*,[58] by the very victories that grace has obtained for it, has become high-minded, clings tighter to what it esteems good, and is even more capable of resisting.[59] God, who is determined to subdue it, uses for that purpose an apparent resurrection of that very nature that the soul believed was dead. But note that He does not use the flesh until He has extracted its evil, destroyed it, and separated the superior will [of the soul] from that which made the flesh violent and criminal. He extracts the venom of the viper, and then uses it as an antidote to *self*. Whoever becomes acquainted with the marvelous economy of grace and the wisdom of God in bringing us to a *total sacrifice of self* will be filled with delight, and, unemotional as that person may be, will be consumed[60] with love. The little traces of it that have been revealed to my heart, have often overwhelmed me with great love and joy.

SUFFERING THE REMOVAL OF EVERYTHING

Faithfulness in this stage requires us to suffer the removal[61] [of everything] to the complete measure of the plans of God [for us]. We must not be anxious about ourselves, but must sacrifice to God all our interests for time and for eternity. Nothing must be made an excuse for reserving or retaining the slightest atom, for the least reservation is the cause of an irreparable loss, because it prevents our death [to self] from being total. We must let God work His absolute pleasure, and suffer the winds and storms to beat upon us from every quarter, even though we will often be submerged beneath the raging waves.

Yet we become aware of a wonderful thing here[62]—far from being separated[63] [from God] by our suffering and miserable[64] state, it is then that God appears. And if any weakness has been apparent, He gives us some token of His immediate presence, as if to assure our soul for a moment that He is with it in its tribulation. I say, *for a moment,* for the sense of His presence gives no continual support,[65] but is rather intended to show us[66] the way and encourage[67] our soul to further loss of *self.*

SOME PERIODS OF RELIEF

These stages are not continually severe—there are periods of relief.[68] Yet, while they give room for taking a breath, they do make the next trial more painful,[69] [because of its comparison to the period of relief, and because we try to hang on to it]. For *self* will make use of anything to keep its life—just as a drowning person would hang on to even a board covered with jagged glass, without concern for the pain, if there was nothing else within reach.[70]

THE FIFTH STAGE: MYSTICAL DEATH [OF THE SOUL][71]

Now attacked on all sides by so many enemies, without life and without support, we have no recourse but to die [to self] in the arms of Love. When death is complete, the most terrible conditions cause no further trouble. We do not recognize death from the fact of having passed through all these stages [and conditions], but by an absolute lack[72] of power to feel pain, or to think of or care for *self.* Also, by our being indifferent to whether we remain there forever without manifesting the slightest sign of vitality. Life is evidenced by liking or disliking something[73]—[love or hate]. But here in this mystical death of the soul,[74] all things are alike. Now being dead, the soul is insensible to everything that concerns it. It no longer matters to the soul how much God reduces [and weakens] it, for it feels nothing.[75] It has no preference[76] between being angel or devil[77] [in God's use of it], because it no longer has any eyes for *self.* It is then that God has placed all the soul's enemies beneath His footstool, and reigning supreme takes and possesses the soul more fully— because the soul has more fully deserted *self.* But this takes place by degrees.

Even after the soul's mystical death, however, there remains for a long time a trace of its natural energy,[78] which is only gradually dissipated. All stages have the effect of cleansing the soul somewhat,[79] but in this stage[80] the process is completed.

Dying to spiritual life of the soul

We do not die spiritually [see note[81]] once for all, as we do naturally. It is accomplished gradually. We alternate[82] between life and death, being sometimes in one and sometimes in the other, until death has finally conquered life. So it is in the resurrection [of the soul]—an alternate state of life and death, until life has finally overcome death.

[It is] not that the new life [of the soul] does not come suddenly. The soul[83] that was dead is now living,[84] and can never afterward doubt that it was dead and is alive again. But it is not yet [fully] established [in the new life]. It has more of a leaning toward living in the new life rather than being firmly settled in it.[85]

First life of grace began in our senses

The first life of grace began in our senses—those things we could perceive, and then sank continually inward toward our center—God. This inward movement continued until our soul was reduced to nothing but itself, and had no help or support from anything. At that point, it died to itself into the arms of Love. For all of us traveling this path experience this death, but by ways different for each of us. The life that is now communicated arises from within [us]. It is, as it were, a living germ[86] that has always existed there, although undetected. This demonstrates that the life of grace was never wholly absent [from us during the process of the soul's death], however it may have been allowed to remain hidden. There it remained even in the midst of death—yet it was not less death because life was concealed in it. It is like the butterfly that lies long dead in the chrysalis, but contains [within itself] a germ of life that awakes it to a resurrection. This new life, then, buds in our center, and grows from there—gradually extends itself over all our faculties and senses, impregnating them with its own life and richness [of productive power].[87]

The soul endued with this vitality experiences an infinite contentment. Not contentment in itself, but in God—especially when the [new] life is well advanced.

But before explaining the effects of this admirable life, let me say that there are some who do not pass through these painful [inner] deaths. They only experience an intense weakness and timidity that reduces them to nothing in themselves and causes them to die to everything.[88]

NOT YET TOTAL DEATH

Many spiritual persons have given the name of death to the earlier purifications. They are, indeed, a death in relation to the life [that is eventually] communicated, but not a total death. They extinguish some of the lives, or activities, of the flesh, or of grace, but that is widely different from the final and general extinction of all life.[89]

[This] death has various names, according to our different ways of speaking of it or our concept of it.[90] It is called a *departure*—that is, a separation from *self* so that we may pass into God. A total and entire *loss* of the person's will, which causes the soul to be totally empty of anything in itself, so that it may exist only in God. Now, as this will is in everything—that is, controls everything—that exists in the person, however good and holy it may be, all these things must necessarily be destroyed. [This destruction must continue] as long as they exist and the [so-called] good will of the person is in them, so that will of God alone remains. Everything born of the will of the flesh and the will of the soul, must be destroyed. Then nothing but the will of God is left, which becomes the [operating] principle [or force] of the new life. [God's will] gradually animates the old extinguished will, takes its place [as the operating principle], and changes it into faith—[that is, the person's resurrected will now lives entirely by the faith of Christ].[91]

From the time that the soul expires mystically, it is separated generally from everything that would be an obstacle to its perfect union with God. But for all that, it is not [yet] received into God. This causes it the most extreme suffering. You will object here, perhaps, that if the soul is completely dead it can no longer suffer. Let me explain.

SOUL IS DEAD WHEN SEPARATED FROM SELF

The soul is dead [to everything] as soon as it is separated from *self*, but this death[92] is not complete until it has passed into God. Until then, it suffers very greatly, but its suffering is general and indistinct, and proceeds solely from the fact that it is not yet established in its proper place.

The suffering that precedes death—[physical death of the body or mystical death of the soul], is caused by our loathing of the ways that are to produce it. This loathing returns whenever those ways recur or grow sharper. But as we die, we become equally more and more insensible, and [even] seem to harden under the blows, until at last death comes in truth through an entire cessation of all life. God has unrelentingly pursued *self*-life [of the soul] into all its secret hiding places, for it is so malignant that when it is hard pressed it fortifies itself in its strongholds. There it makes use of the holiest and most reasonable pretexts for [its continued] existence. But being pursued and followed [by God] into its last retreat, in a few souls (alas! how few!) it is obliged to abandon those pretexts altogether.[93]

There is now no pain coming from the ways that caused the soul's mystical death, and which are exactly the opposite to those ways that were used to maintain our *self*-life—[for example, to destroy pride, humiliation is used]. Now [be aware that] the more reasonable and holy the latter ways seem to be, the more unreasonable and defiled the ways of death will seem to be.[94]

SOUL LOSES EVERYTHING SELF CLAIMED AS ITS OWN

Death separates the soul from *self*, and in so doing causes it to lose everything that *self* ever claimed as its own. Now we never know how strongly we cling to objects until they are taken away. So much so, that if anyone thinks they are not attached to anything, they are frequently greatly mistaken, and are bound to a thousand unknown things. After death, however, the soul is entirely rid of *self*, but not at first received into God. There still exists a something, I do not know exactly what, a form, a human remnant—but that also vanishes. This unknown something, this tarnish on the soul, is destroyed by a general, indistinct, suffering. This suffering, however, has no relation to the ways of death previously mentioned, since they are completed and have passed away. This suffering is rather an uneasiness that arises from the fact of the soul being separated from *self* without being yet received into its Creator. The soul loses all possession of *self*—[or perhaps *self* loses all possession of the soul], for if it did not it could never be united to God. But it is only gradually that the soul becomes fully possessed by Him. This is done by means of the new life, which is completely divine.[95]

UNION WITH GOD—BUT NOT YET RECOGNIZED

As soon as the soul has died in the arms of the Lord, it is united to Him in truth and without any intermediate—[that is, nothing between it and Him]. For in losing everything, even its best possessions, it has lost the means and intermediates that dwelt in them. Even its greatest treasures themselves were but intermediates.[96] The moment the soul dies, therefore, it is united to God immediately. It does not, however, recognize it or enjoy the fruits of its union until He animates it and becomes its vitalizing principle. A bride fainting in the arms of her husband[97] is closely united to him, but she does not enjoy the blessedness of the union, and may even be unconscious of it. When he realizes, however, that she has fainted from excess of love, and restores her to consciousness by his tender caresses, then she perceives that she is in possession of him whom her soul loves, and that she is possessed by him.[98]

PART II

RESULTS OF UNION
WITH GOD

THE RESURRECTION

The soul that is possessed of God finds that He is so perfectly Lord over it that it can no longer do anything but what He pleases and as He pleases, and that this state is continually increasing. Its powerlessness is no longer painful but pleasant, because it is full of the life and power of the divine will.[99]

The dead soul is in union [with God], but it does not enjoy the fruits of it until the moment of its *Resurrection,* when God causes it to pass into Him. [It is then that He] gives it such pledges and assurances of the consummation of its divine marriage that it can no longer doubt [the reality of the union]. For this direct[100] union is so spiritual, so refined, so divine, so intimate, that it is equally impossible for the soul to imagine it[101] as it is to doubt it—because the entire way is infinitely removed from any imagination.[102] These [dead] souls are not in the least imaginative, since nothing in the intellect [affects them any longer], and [so they] are perfectly protected from deceptions and illusions since everything takes place internally.

During their passage through the way of faith, they had nothing distinct, for distinctness is entirely opposed to faith. Therefore, they could not enjoy anything of that sort, having only a certain generality as a foundation upon which everything was communicated to them. But it is far otherwise when the [new] life becomes advanced in God. For though they have nothing distinct for themselves, they do have for others. The light they receive for the use of others, though not always received by those for whom it is intended, is more [distinct and] certain because it is more direct and, as a result, unchanged.[103]

WHEN GOD RECEIVES A SOUL INTO HIMSELF

When God raises a soul—that is to say, receives it into Himself, the living germ, which is no other than the life and Spirit of the Word, begins to appear. [Contained within the Spirit] is *the revelation of Jesus Christ*,[104] who now lives [fully] in us because of the loss of the life of Adam [that formerly] existed in *self*.[105]

The soul is thus received into God, and is there gradually changed and transformed into Him, just as food is transformed into the one who has partaken of it.[106] All this takes place without any loss of the soul's own individual [and distinct] existence, as has been explained elsewhere.

When transformation begins, it is called *annihilation,* since in changing the structure of the soul—[that is, the way it has always done things], we become dead to that way of doing things in order to take on His way.[107] This operation goes on constantly during life, changing the soul more and more into God,[108] and conferring upon it a continually increasing participation in the divine qualities.[109] In so doing, it makes the soul unchangeable, immovable, etc. God also makes the soul fruitful in Him, but not out of Him.

This fruitfulness [normally] extends to certain persons whom God gives and attaches to the soul, communicating to [and through] it His love [for them]— [a love] full of generosity and goodness.[110] For the love of these divine souls[111] for the individuals thus bestowed upon them, while it is far removed from any natural feelings, is infinitely stronger than the love of parents for their children. And though it appears eager and impetuous,[112] it is not. For those who exhibit such love merely follow the movement [of God's love] impressed upon them—[that is, upon their soul].[113]

SOME THINGS WE NEED TO KNOW TO UNDERSTAND

To understand all this, we must know that God did not deprive the senses and faculties of their life and leave them dead. For though there might be life in the center of the soul, the senses and faculties would remain dead if that life were not also communicated to *them*. The communication of that life increases by degrees and animates all the faculties and senses, which until then had remained barren and unfruitful. It enlarges them[114] in proportion to the amount of life communicated, and makes them active, but with an activity derived from God and regulated by Him according to His own designs. Persons [who are still] in a dying or dead condition,[115] must not condemn the activity of such souls, for they could never have been put in divine motion if they had not passed through the most wonderful death. During the whole way [or stage] of faith, the soul remains motionless. But after God has infused into it His divine activity, its area of activity is vastly extended. Great as the activity may be, however, the soul cannot execute a self-originating movement.[116]

THE LIFE IN GOD

There is nothing more to be said here about degrees. The only degree is that of glory, for every means [used to change our soul] is now left behind, and the future consists of our enjoying an infinite stretch of [God's] life, and that more and more abundantly.[117] As God transforms the soul into Himself, His life is communicated to it more plentifully. The love of God for us is incomprehensible, and His persistent pursuit[118] inexplicable. Some souls He pursues without interruption, goes before[119] them, seats Himself at their door, and delights Himself in being with them and in loading them with the signs of His love. He impresses His chaste, pure, and tender love upon the heart. The apostles Paul and John felt this maternal affection the most. But to be as I have described it, it must be bestowed upon the soul in the state of grace, [the union], that I have just spoken about. Otherwise, such emotions are purely natural—[of the flesh and not of the Spirit].[120]

During the stage or way of naked faith, prayer [is almost impossible because] of an absolute deadness of all the faculties[121] of the soul—[it can no longer pray effectively]. Further, it is also impossible to work, however delicately, or pray toward ending that deadness. Not being able to sense that it can pray anymore, or set aside fixed times for prayer, since all such exercises have been taken away, the soul in that state is led to think that it has absolutely lost every kind of devotion [it ever had].[122] But when life returns, prayer returns with it, accompanied by a marvelous easiness [in praying]. As God takes possession of the senses and faculties [of the soul], its devotion becomes sweet, gentle, and very spiritual, but always to God. Its former devotion caused it to sink within itself so that it might enjoy God. But that which it now has, draws it out of itself so that it may be more and more lost and transformed in God.

A REMARKABLE DIFFERENCE

This difference is quite remarkable, and can only be accomplished by experience. In the state of death [previously discussed], the soul is silent, but the silence is barren and is accompanied by a frantic rambling [as the soul desperately tries to pray]. Thus there is no sign of silence, except the [silence created by the] impossibility of addressing God either with the lips or the heart. But after the resurrection, the soul's silence is fruitful and accompanied by an exceedingly pure and refined anointing that is deliciously poured over the senses—poured with such a [holy] purity that nothing can stop its activity or defile it.[123]

It is now impossible for the soul to take what it has not, or to put off what it has. It receives with passive willingness whatever impressions are made upon it. This condition, which is sometimes overwhelming [in its anointing], would be free from suffering if God, who moves us toward certain free things [He has for us], would give us the necessary instructions [on how to receive them]. But since our soul's present passive state could not bring forth [what God has for it], it becomes necessary that what God wills we should have be communicated to us by means[124] of suffering, [which further purifies our soul and moves it even closer to God].[125]

WITHDRAWING FROM GOD'S WAY TO UNION

It would be wrong for persons in this state to say that they do not wish these means, that they desire God only. He desires, however, that they die to a certain interior support that [a remnant] of self [still gives them], and which makes them say that they desire God only. But if they were to reject these means, they would withdraw themselves from God's order—[that is, the sequence in which He moves the soul toward Himself], and stop their progress. The purpose of the suffering is often kept secret and concealed from the person, and though it is fruitful in grace and virtue,[126] it is only a method that God uses. So it is removed when the soul is united with the means in God—[that is, the ways in God Himself that purify the soul], and He communicates Himself directly [to the soul]. God then withdraws the means— no longer moving them toward the person to whom they were attached, [and no longer giving them any ability to move the person any closer to Him]. He does this because the means might now serve as a support, since the person has recognized their purpose. Now the soul cannot have anything it had, and though its previous ways are still closely united to it, it is completely dead to them.[127]

INDESCRIBABLE SILENCE

In this state of resurrection comes that indescribable silence, by which we not only exist in God, but commune[128] with Him. In this state, a soul that is dead to its own working, and to any general and fundamental rights of its own, experiences a divine communication with God flowing freely back and forth. There is now nothing to soil its purity, for there is nothing to hinder it.[129]

Your soul then becomes a partaker of the indescribable communion of the Trinity, where the Father of spirits imparts [to your soul] His spiritual richness and fertility, and makes it one spirit with Himself. Here it is that your soul communes with other souls, according to the stage [of their soul's development] and its condition, and if they are sufficiently pure to receive its communications in silence. Here it is, also, that the indescribable secrets [of God] are revealed, not by a momentary illumination, but in God Himself where they are all hid. Your soul, however, does not possess them for itself, [but for others]—yet it is not ignorant of them.[130]

DISTINCT REVELATIONS OR ILLUMINATIONS

Although I have said that your soul now has something distinct, yet it is not distinct in reference to itself, but to those with whom it communicates. For what you say [verbally] is said naturally and without attention, but seems extraordinary to your listeners. Not finding the thing [about which you speak] in themselves, even though it may be there, they consider it as something distinct and wonderful, or perhaps fanatical. Those who are still living in [natural and spiritual] gifts, have distinct and momentary illuminations. But those who have advanced into God do not have distinct revelations,[131] but only a general illumination, which is God Himself. From Him they draw whatever they need, such as distinct illumination whenever it is required by those with whom they are talking. After they finish their conversation, however, that distinct illumination leaves them.[132]

The Transformation

There are a thousand things that might be said about the inward and heavenly life of the soul that is full of life in God.[133] Such souls He dearly cherishes for Himself, and He continually humbles[134] them externally, because He is a jealous God. But it would require a volume, and I have only to fulfill your request.[135] God is the life and soul of those who now live uninterruptedly in God[136] in inexpressible happiness, [even] though loaded with the sufferings that God lays upon them for others.

[The soul of these blessed ones] has become so simple, especially when its transformation is far advanced, that they go their way continually[137] without a thought for any persons[138] or for themselves. They have but one object, to do the will of God. But since God's will has to do with many of those who cannot attain to this state, some of them cause [these blessed ones] suffering by endeavoring to compel them to have concern for themselves, to take precautions, and so on, which they cannot do. Others do the same toward them because of their lack of [understanding and] conformity[139] to the will of God.

Severe crosses

The crosses of [these blessed] souls are the most severe, and God keeps them under the most abject humiliations and a very common and weak exterior,[140] even though they are His delight. Then Jesus Christ communicates Himself in all His states, and the soul is clothed upon both with His inclinations and sufferings.

The person then understands [as never before] what humanity has cost Christ, what human faithlessness has made Him suffer, what is the redemption of Jesus Christ, and how He has given birth to God's children.

The transformation [of the person's soul] is recognized by the lack of distinction between God and their soul—it is no longer able[141] to separate itself [or act separately] from God. [To the transformed soul] everything is equally God, because it has passed into its Original Source, reunited to its ALL, and changed into Him. But it is enough for me to sketch the general outlines of what you desire to know—experience will teach you the rest.[142] Having [now] shown you what I ought to be to you, you may judge of what I am in our Lord.

EVERYTHING TO YOUR SOUL IS EXTENDED AND EXPANDED

In proportion [to the degree that the] transformation is perfected, the soul finds a more extended quality in itself. Everything is expanded and extended. God has made the soul a partaker of His infinity, so that it often finds itself immense, and the whole earth appears but as a point in comparison with this wonderful breadth and extension. Whatever is in the order and will of God expands it—everything else contracts it, and this contraction restrains it from passing out [of the will of God]. Since our will is the means of effecting the transformation, and the center is nothing else but all the [soul's] faculties united in the will, the more our soul is transformed, the more its will is changed and passed into that of God, and the more God Himself wills for our soul. Our soul acts and works in God's divine will, which is now substituted for its own.

[This is done] so naturally that it is impossible to tell whether the will of our soul has become the will of God, or the will of God has become the will of our soul.

God frequently exacts strange sacrifices from [those whose] souls are transformed in Him. But [the sacrifices] cost them nothing, for they will sacrifice everything to Him without revulsion. The smaller sacrifices cost the most, and the greater ones the least, for the greater sacrifices are not required until our soul is in a state to grant them without difficulty, to which it has a natural tendency. This is what is said of Jesus Christ on His coming into the world: "Then said I, Lo, I come: in the volume of the book it is written of Me, I delight to do Thy will, O my God: yea, Thy law is within My heart."[143] As soon as Christ comes into the soul [of any person] to become its living principle, He says the same thing of it. He becomes the eternal Priest who unceasingly fulfills within the soul His priestly office. This is sublime indeed, and continues until the person is carried to glory.

GOD NOW USES YOU TO HELP OTHERS

God destines these [whose souls have been transformed] for the assistance of others [who are] in the most tangled paths. [Because they] no longer have any anxiety in regard to themselves, nor anything to lose, God can use them to bring others into the way of His pure, naked, and assured will. Those who are still self-possessed could not be used for this purpose. For they have not yet entered into a state where they follow the *will of God blindly* for themselves. They always mingle it with their own reasonings and false wisdom. So they are not by any means in a condition to withhold nothing in following it blindly for others—[by that I mean, giving to others what God has shown is His will for them]. When I say *withhold nothing,* I mean of that which God desires in the present moment. He frequently does not permit us to point out to people all that hinders them, and what we see must come to pass in respect to them, except in general terms, because they cannot bear it. And though we may sometimes say hard things [to a person], as Christ did to those in Capernaum,[144] He nevertheless bestows a secret strength to bear it. At least He does so to the souls [of those] whom He has chosen solely for Himself, and that is the touchstone— [the test of genuineness].

¹ John 17:22

² Original word: *Degree* — In her text, Madame Guyon sometimes uses the word "state" to mean the same thing.

³ Madame Guyon uses the expression, "the soul," which is understood to mean your soul, or you. So to make it more relative, we are using the expression "your soul" wherever she uses "the soul."

⁴ Original subhead: *The Second Degree: the Effectual Touch in the Will*

⁵ John 14:23, Ephesians 3:17

⁶ Original words: *in its very commencement*

⁷ Philippians 2:13 — Original sentences: *This knowledge is the more admirable, as it is the spring of all the felicity of the Soul, and the solid foundation of interior progress; for those Souls who tend toward God merely by the intellect, even though they should enjoy a somewhat spiritual contemplation, yet can never enter into Intimate Union, if they do not quit that path and enter this of the Inward Touch, where the whole working is in the Will.*

⁸ *illuminations*: spiritual or intellectual enlightenment

⁹ Original sentence: *And further, all the more immediate operations are performed in the Centre of the Soul, that is, in the Three Powers reduced to the Unity of the Will, where they are all absorbed, insensibly following the path prescribed for them by that Touch to which we have before referred.*

¹⁰ Original word: *constrains*

¹¹ Original word: *aridities* — probably used in the sense of *lacking interest or feeling.*

¹² Original word: *fix*

[13] Original words: *having more sensible delights, and others being drier*

[14] Original paragraph: *These latter are they who pursue the Way of Faith and absolute Abandonment. They have neither relish nor liberty for any other path; all else constrains and embarrasses them. They dwell in greater aridities than the others, for as there is nothing distinct to which their minds are attached, their thoughts often wander and have nothing to fix them. And as there are differences in Souls, some having more sensible delights, and others being drier, so it is with those who are led by the Will; the former sort have more relish and less solid acquirement, and should restrain their too eager disposition, and suffer their emotions to pass, even when they seem burning with love; the latter seem harder and more insensible, and their state appears altogether natural; nevertheless, there is a delicate something in the depth of the Will, which serves to nourish them, and which is, as it were, the condensed Essence of what the others experience in the intellect and in ardor of purpose.*

[15] Original words: *very inmost recesses*

[16] Original words: *a cold and languid*

[17] Original paragraph: *You will ask me, then, if these Souls are urged on by no violent influence, but walk in blindness, do they do the will of God? They do, more truly, although they have no distinct assurance of it; His Will is engraved in indelible characters on their very inmost recesses, so that they perform with a cold and languid, but firm and inviolable, abandonment, what the others accomplish by the drawings of an exquisite delight.*

[18] Original words: *by a faith more or less sensibly savory*

[19] Original word: *aridity*

[20] Original word: *illumination*

[21] Original word: *luminous*

[22] Original word: *interior*

[23] Words removed after *unable*: *in their insipid way,*

[24] Removed redundant words: *insensibly and*

[25] Original word: *relish*

[26] Original word: *state*

[27] Original words: *these alternations of*

[28] Original word: *transitory*

[29] Original word: *Unction*

[30] Original words: *secures us*

[31] Original word: *endeavoring*

[32] Original word: *respite*

[33] Original words: *life of Nature*

[34] Original word: *repugnances*

[35] Original words: *and in which*

[36] Original words: *contrivance that God does not discover to the Soul,*

[37] Original words: *so that at length, by this constant practice, accompanied by the gracious Unction before referred to,*

[38] Original word: *part*

[39] Original words: *a state of Death*

[40] Original word: *that of the Spirit*

[41] Original words: *and is next in order to the other*

[42] Original paragraph: *When we have for some time enjoyed the repose of a victory that has cost us so much trouble, and suppose ourselves forever relieved from an enemy whose whole power has been destroyed, we enter into the third degree, next in order to the other, which is a Way of Faith more or less savory, according to the state. We enter into a condition of alternate dryness and facility, as I have stated, and in this dryness, the Soul perceives certain exterior weaknesses, natural defects, which, though slight, take it by surprise; it feels, too, that the strength it had received for the struggle, is dying away. This is caused by the loss of our active, inward force; for although the Soul, in the second degree, imagines itself to be in silence before God, it is not entirely so. It does not speak, indeed, either in Heart or by Mouth, but it is in an active striving after God and constant outbreathing of Love, so that, being the subject of the most powerful amorous activity, exerted by the Divine Love towards Himself, it is continually leaping, as it were, towards its object, and its activity is accompanied by a delightful and almost constant Peace. As it is from this activity of Love that we acquire the strength to overcome Nature, it is then that we practice the greatest virtues and most severe mortifications.*

[43] Original paragraph: *But just in proportion as this activity decays, and is lost in a love passivity, so does our strength of resistance sink and diminish. and, as this degree advances, and the Soul becomes more and more passive, it becomes more and more powerless in combat. As God becomes strong within, so do we become weak. Some regard this impossibility of resistance as a great temptation, but they do not see that all our labor, aided and assisted by Grace, can*

only accomplish the conquest of our Outward Senses, after which God takes gradual possession of our Interior, and becomes Himself our purifier. And as He required all our watchfulness while He continued us in amorous activity, so He now requires all our Fidelity to let Him work, while He begins to render Himself Lord by the subjection of the Flesh to the Spirit.

[44] Original words: *For it must be observed*

[45] Original paragraph: *The second degree accomplishes the destruction of the Outward Senses, the third, that of the inward, and this is brought about by means of this savory passivity. But as God is then working within, He seems to neglect the outward, and hence the reappearance of defects, though feebly and only in a time of aridity, which we thought extinct.*

[46] Original sentence: *As soon as we cease, from inability, to practice mortifications of our own fashioning, those of Providence take their place — the crosses which God dispenses according to our degree.*

[47] The word *desolation* is probably used in the sense of *barrenness* or *distressed*.

[48] Original words: *takes place in some with violence*

[49] Original words: *has the appearance*

[50] Romans 7:15

[51] Original paragraph: *After being thus deprived of all things, both inward and outward, which are not essential, the work begins upon those which are; and in proportion as the virtuous life becoming a Christian, which we regarded with so much complacency, disappears, we are likewise spoiled of a certain interior delight and substantial support. As this support becomes weaker and more subtile, the more perceptible*

becomes its loss. It is to be remarked, however, that there is no loss except to our own consciousness, as it still exists in the Soul, but imperceptibly and without apparent action. If it were not hidden, the death and loss of Self could not be accomplished. But it retires within, and shuts itself up so closely that the Soul is not aware of its presence.

[52] Galatians 5:6

[53] Original paragraph: *Do you ask why this course is pursued? The whole object of the Way thus far has been to cause the Soul to pass from multiplicity to the distinct sensible without multiplicity; from the distinct sensible to the distinct insensible; then to the sensible indistinct, which is a general delight much less attractive than the other. It is vigorous in the beginning and introduces the Soul into the perceived, which is a purer and less exquisite pleasure than the first; from the perceived, into Faith sustained and working by Love; passing in this Way from the sensible to the spiritual, and from the spiritual to Naked Faith, which, causing us to be dead to all spiritual experiences, makes us die to ourselves and pass into God, that we may live henceforth from the Life of God only.*

[54] *economy:* Theology—The method of God's government of and activity within the world.

[55] *sensible*: perceptible by the senses or by the mind.

[56] Original paragraph-sentence: *It is stripped without mercy, then, equally and at the same time, of everything both within and without, and what is worst of all, is delivered over to temptations; and the more fully it is thus given up to temptation, the more completely is it deprived of strength to resist them from without; thus it is weakened still farther at the very time when it is*

subjected to more violent attacks, and finally its internal support is removed, which, while it served as a refuge and asylum, would be an evidence of the Goodness of God, and of its Faithfulness to itself.

[57] Original word: *powerlessness*

[58] Original words: *Spirit of Self* — This is the first time Madame Guyon used this expression, and it seems to have no specific meaning. Self does not have a spirit, and so it is impossible to determine what she meant by the expression. A few sentences later, she used another expression "antidote to the Spirit," in which she must have been referring to the "Spirit of Self" that she used here, since she could not have been referring to an antidote for the Holy Spirit or even for our spirit. So that expression has been changed to read, "antidote to self."

[59] Original sentence: *You will, perhaps, remind one that I have before stated that, in the first contest of amorous activity, Nature and the Senses had become, as it were, extinguished and subdued. It is true; but the Spirit of Self, by the very victories that Grace had thus acquired for it, has become high-minded, more tenacious of what it esteems good, and still more indomitable.*

[60] Original word: *expire*

[61] Original word: *spoliation*

[62] Original words: *A wonderful thing is here perceived;*

[63] Original word: *estranged*

[64] Original word: *wretched*

[65] Original words: *is of no service subsequently, as a*

[66] Original words: *point out*

[67] Original word: *invite*

[68] Original words: *These states are not continuous in their violence; there are remissions*

[69] Original words: *and, which, while they afford space for taking breath, serve, at the same time, to render the subsequent trial more painful.*

[70] Original sentence: *For Nature will make use of anything to sustain its life, as a drowning man will support himself in the water by clinging to the blade of a razor, without adverting to the pain it causes him, if there be nothing else within his reach.*

[71] Madame Guyon is undoubtedly using "mystical death" in the sense that the death of the soul is a spiritual reality even though it is not apparent to the senses or intelligence—especially of others.

[72] Original word: *want*

[73] Original words: *a Will for or repugnance to*

[74] When *self* is destroyed and separated by its destruction from the soul, the soul dies in the sense that it is no longer affected by all those things that affected it when *self* was alive and active. It is much like when a person dies and the soul of the person is by that death separated from the body. The soul can no longer be affected by anything that happens to the body, or by anything of the world that affected it through the body.

[75] Original words: *and, let God reduce it to what extremity He will, feels no repugnance.*

[76] Original word: *choice*

[77] By this it is understood that Madame Guyon means being seen by others as an angel or a devil in things that God has the person do. Madame Guyon was called an angel by thousands of people that she helped, and called a devil by thousands in her church, especially the clergy.

[78] Original words: *the living heat*

[79] Original words: *states effect somewhat towards cleansing the Soul*

[80] Original word: *here*

81 Madame Guyon cannot mean here that we die spiritually in the scriptural sense, for spiritual death is separation from God. So she must mean that we die to the spiritual life of our soul—that is, to its self-efforts to live a spiritual life.

[82] Original word: *vibrate*

[83] Original word: *He*

[84] Original words: *finds himself living*

[85] Original words: *is rather a disposition toward living, then a settled state of life.*

[86] *living germ*: used in the sense of something that may serve as the basis of further growth or development.

[87] Original paragraph: *The first life of Grace began in the sensible, and sank continually inward toward the Centre, until, having reduced the Soul to Unity, it caused it to expire in the arms of Love; for all experience this death, but each by means peculiar to himself. But the life that is now communicated arises from within; it is, as it were, a living germ which has always existed there, though unobserved, and which demonstrates that the life of Grace has never been wholly absent, however it may have been suffered to remain hidden. There it remained even in the midst of death; nor was it less death because life was concealed in it; as the silk-worm lies long dead in the chrysalis, but contains a germ of life that awakes it to a resurrection. This new life, then, buds in the Centre, and grows from there; thence it gradually extends over*

all the faculties and senses, impregnating them with its own life and fecundity.

[88] Original sentence: *they only experience a mortal languor and fainting, which annihilate them, and cause them to die to all.*

[89] Original sentence: *They result in an extinguishment of some one of the lives of Nature, or of Grace; but that is widely different from a general extinction of all life.*

[90] Original words: *manner of expression or conception*

[91] Galatians 2:20 — Original paragraph: *Death has various names, according to our different manner of expression or conception. It is called a departure, that is, a separation from Self in order that we may pass into God; a loss, total and entire, of the Will of the creature, which causes the Soul to be wanting to itself, that it may exist only in God. Now, as this Will is in everything that subsists in the creature, however good and holy it may be, all these things must necessarily be destroyed, so far as they so subsist, and so far as the good will of man is in them, that the Will of God alone may remain. Everything born of the will of the flesh and the will of man, must be destroyed. Then nothing but the Will of God is left, which becomes the principle of the new life, and, gradually animating the old extinguished will, takes its place and changes it into Faith.*

[92] Words removed: *or mystic decease*

[93] Original paragraph: *The suffering which precedes death, is caused by our repugnance to the means that are to produce it. This repugnance returns whenever these means recur, or grow sharper; but in proportion as we die we become more and more insensible, and*

seem to harden under the blows, until at last death comes in truth through an entire cessation of all life. God has unrelentingly pursued our life into all its covert hiding places; for so malignant is it, that when hard pressed, it fortifies itself in its refuges, and makes use of the holiest and most reasonable pretexts for existence; but, being persecuted and followed into its last retreat, in a few souls (alas! how few!) it is obliged to abandon them altogether.

[94] Original paragraph: *No pain then remains arising from the means which have caused our death, and which are exactly the opposite to those which used to maintain our life; the more reasonable and holy the latter are in appearance, the more unreasonable and defiled is the look of the other.*

[95] Original paragraph: *But after death — which is the cause of the Soul's departure from Self, that is, of its losing every Self-appropriation whatever; for we never know how strongly we cling to objects until they are taken away, and he who thinks that he is attached to nothing, is frequently grandly mistaken, being bound to a thousand things, unknown to himself — after death, I repeat, the Soul is entirely rid of Self, but not at first received into God. There still exists a something, I know not exactly what, a form, a human remnant; but that also vanishes. It is a tarnish which is destroyed by a general, indistinct suffering, having no relation to the means of death, since they are passed away and completed; but it is an uneasiness arising from the fact of being turned out of Self, without being received into its great Original. The Soul loses all possession of Self, without which it could never be united to God; but it is only gradually that it becomes fully possessed of Him by means of the new life, which is wholly divine.*

[96] Things, ways, or means by which the soul communicated with God.

[97] In Madame Guyon's day, it was not uncommon for woman to faint during highly emotional times—not a common occurrence today.

[98] Original paragraph: *As soon as the Soul has died in the embraces of the Lord, it is united to Him in truth and without any intermediate; for in losing everything, even its best possessions, it has lost the means and intermediates which dwelt in them; and even these greatest treasures themselves were but intermediates. It is, then, from that moment, united to God immediately, but it does not recognize it, nor does it enjoy the fruits of its Union, until He animates it and becomes its vivifying principle. A bride fainting in the arms of her husband, is closely united to him, but she does not enjoy the blessedness of the union, and may even be unconscious of it; but when he has contemplated her for some time, fainting from excess of love, and recalls her to life by his tender caresses, then she perceives that she is in possession of him whom her Soul loves, and that she is possessed by him.*

[99] Ephesians 3:19, Philippians 2:13

[100] Original word: *immediate* — This word was undoubtedly used to mean nothing interposed between the soul and God.

[101] Original word: *conceive*

[102] Original sentence: *For we may observe that the whole way whereof we speak, is infinitely removed from any imagination;*

[103] Original word: *natural* — Most likely to mean that because of the direct communication with God, it is

not altered, treated, or disguised by anything intermediate.

[104] Galatians 1:16

[105] Original sentence: *When God raises a Soul, that is to say, receives it into Himself, and the living germ, which is no other than the Life and Spirit of the Word, begins to appear, it constitutes the Revelation in it of Jesus Christ, (Gal. i. 16,) who lives in us by the loss of the life of Adam subsisting in Self.*

[106] 2 Peter 1:4

[107] Original sentence: *When transformation begins, it is called annihilation, since in changing our form, we become annihilated as to our own, in order to take on His.*

[108] By this, Madame Guyon does not mean that our soul actually becomes God, but that the life and will of our soul is absorbed into the life and will of God, so that His life and will become ours—the operating principle and energy of our soul.

[109] Philippians 1:6, 2:13

[110] Original word: *charity*

[111] Divine only in the sense that it is now full of the divine nature of God — see Paul's prayer in Ephesians 4:14-21, in which he says, ". . . that ye might be filled with all the fulness of God."

[112] Original word: *precipitate* — Could also mean in its usage, among other things, *sudden.*

[113] Original paragraph: *This fruitfulness extends to certain persons whom God gives and attaches to the Soul, communicating to it His Love, full of Charity. For the love of these divine Souls for the persons thus bestowed upon them, while it is far removed from the*

natural feelings, is infinitely stronger than the love of parents for their children, and though it appears eager and precipitate, it is not so, because he, who exhibits it, merely follows the movement impressed upon him.

[114] Most likely means enlarges the spiritual sensitivity and abilities of the senses and faculties, since it is God's nature that is communicated to them.

[115] Not physically, but spiritually or mystically, as Madame Guyon calls it.

[116] Original paragraph: *To make this intelligible, we must know that God did not deprive the senses and faculties of their life, to leave them dead; for though there might be life in the Centre of the Soul, they would remain dead if that life were not also communicated to them. It increases by degrees, animates all the powers and senses which, until then, had remained barren and unfruitful, enlarges them in proportion to its communication, and renders them active, but with an activity derived and regulated from God, according to His own designs. Persons in a dying or dead condition, must not condemn the activity of such Souls, for they could never have been put in divine motion if they had not passed through the most wonderful death. During the whole period of Faith, the Soul remains motionless; but after God has infused into it the Divine Activity, its sphere is vastly extended; but, great as it may be, it cannot execute a Self-originated movement.*

[117] John 10:10b — The Greek word translated *life* in this verse is *zoe*, which means "life as God has it — self-existing life — God's quality of life." It is the same Greek word that is translated life in John 5:26, where Jesus said, "For as the Father hath life in Himself; so hath He given to the Son to have life in Himself."

MADAME GUYON

[118] Original word: *assiduity*

[119] Original word: *prevents* — probably used in the archaic meaning *to come before, to precede,* or *to anticipate.*

[120] Original paragraph: *There is no more to be said here of degrees; that of Glory being all that remains, every means being left behind, and the future consisting in our enjoying an infinite stretch of life, and that more and more abundantly. (John x. 10.) As God transforms the Soul into Himself, His life is communicated to it more plentifully. The Love of God for the creature is incomprehensible, and His assiduity inexplicable; some Souls He pursues without intermission, prevents them, seats Himself at their door, and delights Himself in being with them and in loading them with the marks of His Love. He impresses this chaste, pure, and tender love upon the Heart. St. Paul and St. John the Evangelist, felt the most of this maternal affection. But to be as I have described it, it must be bestowed upon the Soul in the state of Grace of which I have just spoken; otherwise, such emotions are purely natural.*

[121] *powers*: the ability or capacity to perform or act effectively.

[122] Original sentences: *The prayer of the state of Faith is an absolute silence of all the powers of the Soul, and a cessation of every working, however delicate, especially toward its termination. The Soul in that state, perceiving no more prayer, and not being able to set apart fixed seasons for it, since all such exercises are taken away, is led to think that it has absolutely lost all kind of devotion.*

[123] Original paragraph: *The Soul is silent in the state of death, but its stillness is barren, and accompanied by*

216

a frantic rambling, which leaves no mark of silence save the impossibility of addressing God, either with the lips or the heart. But after the Resurrection, its silence is fruitful and attended by an exceedingly pure and refined Unction, which is deliciously diffused over the senses, but with such a purity, that it occasions no stay and contracts no taint.

[124] *means*: a method, a course of action, or an instrument by which an act can be accomplished or an end achieved.

[125] "Though He were a Son, yet learned He obedience by the things which He suffered" (Hebrews 5:8). — Original sentences: *Its state, however overwhelming, would be free from suffering, if God, who moves it towards certain free things, gave them the necessary correspondence. But as their state will not bear it, it becomes necessary that what God wills they should have, should be communicated by means of suffering for them.*

[126] *virtue*: moral excellence and righteousness; goodness.

[127] Original paragraph: *It would be wrong for such persons to say that they do not wish these means; that they desire God only. He is anxious that they should die to a certain interior support of Self, which causes them to say that they desire God only, and if they were to reject these means, they would withdraw themselves from the order of God, and arrest their progress. But, being given simply as means, though fruitful in grace and virtue, however secret and concealed, they finally disappear when the Soul finds itself united with the means in God, and He communicates Himself directly. Then God withdraws the means, upon which He no*

longer impresses any movement in the direction of the person to whom they are attached; because it might then serve as a stay, its utility being at last recognized. The Soul can then no longer have what it had, and remains in its first death in respect to them, though still very closely united.

[128] *commune*: to be in a state of intimate, heightened sensitivity and receptivity, as with one's surroundings.

[129] Original paragraph: *In this state of Resurrection comes that ineffable silence, by which we not only subsist in God, but commune with Him, and which, in a Soul thus dead to its own working, and general and fundamental Self-appropriation, becomes a flux and reflux of Divine Communion, with nothing to sully its purity; for there is nothing to hinder it.*

[130] Original paragraph: *The Soul then becomes a partaker of the ineffable communion of the Trinity, where the Father of Spirits imparts His spiritual fecundity, and makes it one Spirit with Himself. Here it is that it communes with other Souls, if they are sufficiently pure to receive its communications in silence, according to their degree and state; here, that the ineffable secrets are revealed, not by a momentary illumination, but in God Himself, where they are all hid, the Soul not possessing them for itself, nor being ignorant of them.*

[131] A revelation or illumination that is clearly defined and easily distinguishable from all others, such as your natural thoughts or feelings.

[132] Original paragraph: *Although I have said that the Soul then has something distinct, yet it is not distinct in reference to itself, but to those with whom it communes; for what it says is said naturally and without*

attention, but seems extraordinary to the hearers, who, not finding the thing in themselves, notwithstanding it may be there, consider it as something distinct and wonderful, or perhaps fanatical. Souls that are still dwelling among gifts, have distinct and momentary illuminations, but these latter have only a general illumination, without defined beams, which is God Himself; whence they draw whatever they need, which is distinct whenever it is required by those with whom they are conversing, and without any of it remaining with themselves afterwards.

[133] John 10:10b; Ephesians 3:19, 5:18

[134] *humble*: to deprive of esteem, self-worth, or effectiveness.

[135] Madame Guyon wrote this detailed explanation of the soul's journey into union with God in response to a request from Fénelon, Archbishop of Cambray, to more clearly explain her teaching that by inner prayer such a union could be accomplished, and the progression of that union. Her letter at that time was titled, *A Concise View of the Soul's Return to God, and of its Re-union with Him.* Whether she succeeded in clarifying her teaching is up to the reader to decide. Fénelon himself wrote a long letter to Madame Guyon in reply, in which he said, "I think, Madame, that I understand, in general, the statements in the paper which you had the kindness to send to me; in which you describe the various experiences which characterize the soul's return to God by means of simple or pure faith." He then detailed the points he thought he understood. We have included a summary of his letter in its original form, with only minor editing, at the end of this section.

[136] The words, *as a fish in the sea,* were removed after *God* because they interrupted the thought.

[137] Original word: *perpetually*

[138] By this Madame Guyon undoubtedly means without a thought or concern of what others think or say about them or try to guide them into a different direction.

[139] Original words: *want of correspondence*

[140] By *weak exterior* Madame Guyon doesn't necessarily mean physically weak, although that may have been somewhat in her thinking since she was always ill and weak in some way. She is more likely referring, however, to lack of external strength in combating or resisting those who come against these advanced souls—no longer having a strong personality in themselves for themselves, if you will.

[141] Original words: *it not being able any longer*

[142] Madame Guyon is here referring to Fénelon, as indicated in a previous note.

[143] Psalm 40:7-8, Hebrews 10:7

[144] Matthew 11:23-24

FÉNELON'S REPLY
TO MADAME GUYON

FÉNELON'S REPLY

Paris, August 11, 1689.

To Madame De La Mothe Guyon, — I think, Madame, that I understand, in general, the statements in the paper that you had the kindness to send to me, in which you describe the various experiences that characterize the soul's return to God by means of simple or pure faith. I will endeavor, however, to summarize some of your views, as they present themselves to me, that I may learn whether I correctly understand them.

1. The first step that is taken by the soul that has formally and permanently given itself to God, would be to bring what may be called its external powers—that is, its natural appetites and propensities, under subjection. The religious state of the soul at such times is characterized by that simplicity that shows its sincerity, and that it is sustained by faith. So that the soul does not act of itself alone, but follows and cooperates, with all its power, with that grace that is given it. It gains the victory through faith.

2. The second step is to cease to rest on the pleasures of inward sensibility. The struggle here is, in general, more severe and prolonged. It is hard to die to

these inward tastes and relishes, which make us feel so happy, and which God usually permits us to enjoy and to rest upon in our first experience. When we lose our inward happiness, we are very apt to think that we lose God—not considering that the moral life of the soul does not consist in pleasure, but in union with God's will, whatever that may be. The victory here also is by faith—acting, however, in a little different way.

3. Another step is that of entire crucifixion to any reliance upon our virtues, either outward or inward. The habits of the life of *self* have become so strong, that there is hardly anything in which we do not take a degree of complacency. Having gained the victory over its senses, and having gained so much strength that it can live by faith, independently of inward pleasurable excitements, the soul begins to take a degree of satisfaction, which is secretly a selfish one, in its virtues, in its truth, temperance, faith, benevolence, and to rest in them as if they were its own—and as if they gave it a claim of acceptance on the ground of its merit. We are to be dead to them, considered as coming from ourselves, and alive to them only as the gifts and the power of God. We are to have no perception or life in them, in the sense of taking a secret satisfaction in them, and are to take satisfaction in the Giver of them only.

4. A fourth step consists in a cessation or death to that revulsion that people naturally feel to those dealings of God that are involved in the process of inward crucifixion. The plows that God sends upon us are received without the opposition that once existed, and existed oftentimes with great power. So clear is the soul's perception of God's presence in everything, and so strong is its faith, that those apparently adverse dealings, once exceedingly trying, are now received not

merely with acquiescence,[1] but with cheerfulness. It kisses the hand that smites it.

5. When we have proceeded so far, the natural man is dead. And then comes, as a fifth step in this process, the *new life*—not merely the *beginning,* but a new life in the higher sense of the terms, the resurrection *of the life of love.* All those gifts that the soul before sought in its own strength, and perverted and rendered poisonous and destructive to itself, by thus seeking them out of God, are now richly and fully returned to it, by the great Giver of all things. It is not the design or plan of God to deprive His creatures of happiness, but only to pour the cup of bitterness into all that happiness, and to smite all that joy and prosperity that the creature has in anything *out of Himself.*

6. And this life, in the sixth place, becomes a truly transformed life, a *life in union with God,* when the will of the soul becomes not only conformed to God practically and in fact, but is conformed to Him in everything in it, and in the relations it sustains, which may be called *a disposition* or *tendency.* It is then that there is such a harmony between the human and Divine will, that they may properly be regarded as having become one. This, I suppose, was the state of St. Paul, when he says, "I live; yet not I, but Christ liveth in me."[2]

It is not enough to be merely passive under God's dealings. The spirit of entire submission is a great grace. But it is a still higher attainment to become *flexible*— that is to say, to move just as He would have us move. This state of mind might perhaps be termed the spirit of *cooperation,* or of *Divine* cooperation. In this state the will is not only subdued, but, what is very important, all tendency to a different or rebellious state is taken away. Of such a soul, which is described as the Temple of the Holy Ghost,[3] God Himself is the inhabitant and the light.

This transformed soul does not cease to advance in holiness. It is transformed without remaining where it is—new without being stationary. Its life is love, *all* love, but the capacity of its love continually increases.

Such, Madame, if I understand them, are essentially the sentiments of the letter that you had the kindness to send me.

I wish you to write me whether the statement that I have now made corresponds with what you intended to convey.

I would make one or two remarks further in explanation of what has been said. One of the most important steps in the process of inward restoration is to be found in the habits of the will. This I have already alluded to, but it is not generally well understood. A person may, perhaps, have a new life, but it cannot be regarded as a *perfectly transformed* life, a life brought into perfect harmony with God, until all the evil influences of former habits are corrected. When this takes place, it is perhaps not easy to determine, but must be left to each one's consciousness. This process must take place in the will, as well as in other parts of the mind. The action of the will must not only be free and right, but must be relieved from all tendency in another direction resulting from previous evil habits.

Another remark that I have to make, is in relation to faith. That all this great work is by faith, is true. But I think we should be careful, in stating the doctrine of faith, not to place it in opposition to reason. On the contrary, we only say what is sustained both by St. Paul and St. Augustine, when we assert that it is a very *reasonable thing to believe.* Faith is different from mere physical and emotive[4] impulse, and it would be no small mistake to accuse those who walk by faith as being thoughtless and impulsive persons and enthusiasts.

Faith is necessarily based upon preceding acts of intelligence. By the use of those powers of perception and reasoning, which God has given us, we have the knowledge of the existence of God. It is by their use also, that we know that God has spoken to us in His revealed Word. In that Word, which we thus receive and verify by reason, we have general truths laid down, general precepts communicated, applicable to our situation and duties. But these truths, coming from Him who has a right to direct us, are authoritative. They *command.* And it is our province and duty, in the exercise of *faith* in the goodness and wisdom of Him who issues the command, to yield obedience, and to go wherever it may lead us, however dark and mysterious the path may now appear. Those who walk by faith walk in obscurity, but they know that there is a light above them, which will make all clear and bright in its appropriate time. We trust—but, as St. Paul says, *we know in whom we have trusted.*[5]

I illustrate the subject, Madame, in this way. I suppose myself to be in a strange country. There is a wide forest before me, with which I am totally unacquainted, although I must pass through it. I accordingly select a guide, whom I suppose to be able to conduct me through these ways never before trodden by me. In following this guide, I obviously go by *faith.* But as I know the character of my guide, and as my intelligence or reason tells me that I ought to exercise such faith, it is clear that my faith in Him is not in opposition to reason, but is in accordance with it. On the contrary, if I refuse to have faith in my guide, and undertake to make my way through the forest by my own shrewdness and wisdom, I may properly be described as a person without reason, or as unreasonable. And I would probably suffer for my lack of reason by losing my way. Faith and reason, therefore, if not identical, are not in disagreement.

Fully subscribing, with these explanations, to the doctrine of faith as the life and guide of the soul, I remain, Madame, yours in our common Lord, Francis S. Fenelon.

[1] *acquiescence*: passive assent or agreement without protest.

[2] Galatians 2:20

[3] 1 Corinthians 6:19

[4] *emotive*: of or relating to emotion.

[5] 2 Timothy 1:12

INDEX OF SUBHEADS